KIT/12
ZLE

Waking With Praise

Paul Iles is a Canon Residentiary and Precentor of Hereford Cathedral where he has been responsible for developing much fresh and imaginative liturgy. He previously worked in parishes in the dioceses of Oxford and Bristol.

He is the author of *Approaching Light – readings and prayers for Advent and Christmas*, published by the Canterbury Press; *The Pleasure of God's Company – a handbook for leading intercession*, published by Kevin Mayhew and *Touching the Far Corners – an exploration of prayer and mission*, published by the Bible Society.

CW00684594

Waking With Praise

Meditations and prayers
for Holy Week, Easter
and the Great Fifty Days

Paul Iles

Illustrated by Gillian Bell-Richards

CANTERBURY
PRESS
Norwich

Bible verses are taken from the New English Bible, the
Revised Standard Version, the Authorized Version and are
sometimes the author's own translation.

Quotations from the Psalms are taken from *The Liturgical
Psalter: new inclusive language version*, published by
HarperCollins.

First published in 1998 by The Canterbury Press Norwich
(a publishing imprint of Hymns Ancient & Modern Limited,
a registered charity)
St Mary's Works, St Mary's Plain,
Norwich, Norfolk NR3 3BH

British Library Cataloguing in Publication Data

A catalogue record for this book is available
from the British Library

ISBN 1-85311-197-X

*Typeset by David Gregson Associates, Beccles, Suffolk
Printed in Great Britain by Biddles Ltd, Guildford and King's Lynn*

For Michael
and the people of Tewkesbury
who invited me to share Good Friday with them
and
for Simon
who persuaded me to write it down.

Contents

Contents

A brighter dawn is breaking,
And earth with praise is waking;
For thou, O King most highest,
The power of death defiest.

And thou hast come victorious,
Wth risen Body glorious,
And now for ever livest,
And life abundant givest.

O free the world from blindness,
And fill the world with kindness,
Give sinners resurrection,
Bring striving to perfection.

In sickness give us healing,
In doubt thy clear revealing,
That praise to thee be given
In earth as in thy heaven.

Percy Dearmer (1867–1936)

Foreword

I can't be the only person who finds praying difficult. I'm too busy, I'm in a hurry, I incline to the infantile, I'm ashamed of my incompetence:

'… How am I going to get to Bromsgrove tomorrow? … I nearly forgot poor Peter … Oh help – it's nearly Lent! What am I to do about Lent? …'

'*Listen* – don't babble!'

So I listen, and I can hear … my heart beat; off again via the Hospice and Bosnia and the children I saw being screamed at in the supermarket, and then I do have to stop to get breakfast.

Life is often a really disorganized mess, and it's shot through too with fairly fundamental doubts and questions. What am I actually doing for Peter if I do remember to pray for him? And anyway, why are there diseases and accidents in the world which we call God's? We'll need to come back to that.

This book by Paul Iles has not wrought a complete and miraculous cure for my incompetence, but it has helped. How? First, by providing a structure. Clearly, there are people who can manage with minimal structure in prayer. They can somehow slide into the consciousness of God's presence almost at will. Perhaps this is because they are always aware of God at a subconscious level. I don't mean to imply that prayer is always easy for them – far from it – but perhaps their difficulties aren't quite of the 'Which is the best road for Bromsgrove?' order. For muddlers like me, a set structure helps. It gives me something to hang on to when my mind is trying to escape from the whole enterprise.

The author makes it possible for me to pace myself rather in the way that knowing the country in which you are walking helps you to pace yourself. The songs and poems and reflections also surprise, sometimes entrance you in the way distant views or sudden turns in the path or shafts of sunlight delight you in country which is only half familiar.

'Sometimes a light surprises the Christian as he sings.' Sometimes perhaps, but not very often in this Christian's experience. But this book does let in light, and the two characteristics of structure and surprise go a long way in the battle against the fearful demon of our time, that hydra demon with several heads, two of which are called Boredom and Distraction.

Pictures of St Anthony's temptation in the desert show him assailed by ghastly demons. I think the ones he was most fearful of are likely to have been sins of the flesh, including Sloth. Sloth has changed his dress a bit now and has called himself Boredom, cleverly suggesting that the sin of Boredom is wholly in the boring, not the bored. Paul Iles charms us out of boredom, and the structure of the prayer disposes us to be won over – putting us in the way of being charmed.

It is also a helpful structural decision of the author to take us beyond Holy Week and Easter to Ascension and Pentecost – reclaiming the Great Fifty Days for our spiritual lives. If this mutes the sighs of relief at the end of Lent, that's a good thing – because what we are looking for is a way through the most important part of the life of Jesus on earth to a closer

experience and understanding of the nature of God and his
extraordinary purposes. We are not looking for a spiritual
assault course in Lent, to be followed by a period of cheerful
indulgence, which tapers off a bit in the discomfort of trying
not to think too hard about whatever the Ascension can
mean.

The Christian Year can become so familiar a pattern that
we are no longer discoverers as we go through it. If we are not
careful, we fragment the history of our redemption into
'manageable' periods, thereby losing meaning and the possibility of discovery. If the book's structure of daily prayer
charms us out of boredom and disorganization, its overall
structure of Holy Week and Pentecost makes us open to
discovery during the Great Fifty Days.

Boredom, unthinking familiarity and unquestioning frag-
mentation all work against our progress in prayer, and as well
as this, in many of us there is an uncomfortable current of
doubt and questioning. This can be creative and life-giving,
however uncomfortable, but it needs to be recognized, faced
and worked on. Too often a vague reluctance to pray can arise
from unacknowledged doubt of the reality and the goodness
of God. Part Three of *Waking with Praise*, and perhaps
especially the section which deals with 'The evilness of evil',
really tries to come to grips with this Great Doubt. Though it
seems more and more that there is no Answer and that we are
faced with mystery wherever we turn, Paul Iles' wrestling
with the experience is a great help, as it refuses easy answers
and suggests directions which lead not to a dead end but to
the discovery of meaning within what has been called 'a
cloud of unknowing'. A cloud of *un*knowing – yes, but
always a bright cloud, or at any rate, a cloud that clears to
give illumination and moments of brightness.

A friend had, in her words, 'made a Good Lent'. On Easter

morning, after church, she was walking home, knowing herself to be happy rather than feeling it. When she passed the URC church she noticed a six-year-old sitting on the steps, taking a little time off from the service. He called out to her, 'Good News Today!' Good news indeed – Alleluia. This book reminds us, refreshes us and recreates our receptivity for the great Good News at the heart of Christian faith and at the centre of the Great Fifty Days.

Meriel Oliver
Bishop's House, Hereford
October 1997

Introduction

One of my colleagues used to say, 'Tell me how a person prays, and I will tell you what kind of God he or she believes in.' It was his way of expressing the principle *lex orandi, lex credendi* – the rules of prayer produce the rules (or structures) of belief. That is where this collection of prayers and meditations begins. It assumes that praying determines believing rather than that believing determines praying. Critics will call that an over-simplification, and probably the two are so enmeshed that they cannot be so easily distinguished, with one given priority over the other. But no one has to look very far to know that beliefs, especially Christian beliefs, can often be hesitant and unclear because prayers remain vague, unimaginative and ill digested. Where prayer is open, adventurous and receptive, the intellect moves better through questions to thoughts which are worth pondering and considering in depth, and which will at length produce at least the start of possible answers in matters of belief.

In a previous book[1] I tried to explore some of the areas available for personal praying which we miss and misuse simply because we mislabel them. Often we pray without realizing it, and without calling it prayer, because no one has yet helped us adequately to say what prayer is. My suggestion was that we should claim back into our prayers the vast areas of daily experience which we have let slip away but which still contain our deepest longings, our thrilling apprehensions of the sacred, our dimly but persistently felt aspirations for healing and fulfilment – in a phrase, our search for God. That is the way of praying to which I respond, and here I have focused it on the experience which brought Christianity into being – Easter and the resurrection.

I have always been grateful that, without quite knowing what I was doing, one of the first books of theology I ever came across and bought was Michael Ramsey's study, *The Resurrection of Christ*. I cannot forget how he begins:

> We are tempted to believe that, although the Resurrection may be the climax of the Gospel, there is yet a Gospel that stands upon its own feet and may be understood and appreciated before we pass on to the Resurrection. The first disciples did not find it so. For them the Gospel without the Resurrection was not merely a Gospel without its final chapter: it was not a Gospel at all.[2]

The prayers and meditations in this book attempt to provide a firm hold on that starting point and invite us to explore the central experience of Christian faith – the dying and rising of Christ.

Provision is made for a scheme of praying during Holy Week and continuing into Easter. The basic ingredients of what might be called 'Offices' are Bible readings, songs (psalms and poems) and prayers with brief meditations. These are the usual ingredients which Christians have used in various ways in both public and private daily prayers. Basic skeleton shapes for using them might be, for example, a Bible reading, a time of prayer, and reading a meditation; or using a song, reading a meditation, followed by prayer. Sometimes you might wish only to use the opening paragraph, 'Beginning to pray', with silence and a concluding prayer.

I hope you will find the material offered flexible enough for you to put it into any shape you feel comfortable with in your own prayers. There is too much rather than too little – but that is deliberate. In praying we need to get used to options and making choices: discarding what we cannot use, recovering what we thought we had grown out of, creating and responding to the shapes and patterns which we build up for ourselves and which meet our personal need at a particular time.

Part One and Part Two of this book consist of prayers and meditations. Part Three is an invitation to think further *after praying*, to follow through some of the foundations which our prayers have begun to establish in heart and mind. The extended essay is intended to reveal how praying and believing fit together, how prayers require further theological reflection, and how theology always needs more prayer.

I am grateful to Christine Smith for her help with the publication of this book. Her patience and encouragement have carried me forward at every stage. I am also grateful to Meriel Oliver for writing her sympathetic Foreword providing personal insights into how Christians might pray the gospel of Easter, and I am delighted to be able to use the illustrations so kindly provided by Gillian Bell-Richards from the remarkable collection of her paintings.

Paul Iles
Hereford
St Luke's Day 1997

Part One
Holy Week

The Road to the End

It has been a long journey,
and my last words shall be these –
that it is only from the inmost
silences of the heart that we know
the world for what it is, and
ourselves for what the world has
made us

Siegfried Sassoon (1886–1967)

Palm Sunday

The pilgrim road into the world and to God

Beginning to pray

Any vision, when its full power
grips imagination and will,
moves us so much
that we go forward,
brave, courageous, disregarding and often heedless;
all that matters is what lies ahead,
calling us on and on,
nearer to the one thing we desire and hope for.
Therefore we need care to allow God
to purge our desires of what is false and destructive,
to fix our attention on him,
on his kingdom
and on all that is good.

Psalm

God is our refuge and strength:
a very present help in trouble.
Therefore we will not fear, though the earth be moved:
and though the mountains are shaken
    in the midst of the sea;

Though the waters rage and foam:
and though the mountains quake at the rising of the sea.
There is a river whose streams make glad the city of God:
the holy dwelling-place of the Most High.
God is in the midst of her,
     therefore she shall not be moved:
God will help her, and at break of day.
The nations make uproar, and the kingdoms are shaken:
But God has lifted his voice, and the earth shall tremble.
The Lord of hosts is with us:
the God of Jacob is our stronghold.

Psalm 46:1–7

Bible reading

Jesus and the disciples were now approaching Jerusalem, and when they reached Bethphage and Bethany, at the Mount of Olives, he sent two of his disciples with these instructions: 'Go to the village opposite, and, just as you enter, you will find tethered there a colt which no one has yet ridden. Untie it and bring it here. If anyone asks, "Why are you doing that", say, "Our Master needs it, and will send it back here without delay." ' So they went off, and found the colt tethered at a door outside in the street. They were untying it when some of the bystanders asked, 'What are you doing, untying that colt?' They answered as Jesus had told them, and were then allowed to take it. So they brought the colt to Jesus and spread their cloaks on it, and he mounted. And people carpeted the road with their cloaks, while others spread brushwood which they had cut in the fields; and those who went ahead and others who came behind shouted, 'Hosanna! Blessings on him who comes in the name of the Lord! Blessings on the coming kingdom of our father David! Hosanna in the heavens!'

Mark 11:1–10

Song

> Travelling the road to freedom,
> Who wants to travel the road with me?
> Fêted by noise and branches
> And banners hanging from every tree;
> Cheered on by frenzied people,
> Puzzled by what they hear and see;
> *Travelling the road to freedom,*
> *Who wants to travel the road with me?*
>
> Travelling the road to freedom,
> Who wants to travel the road with me?
> Partnered by staunch supporters,
> Who, come the dark, will turn and flee;
> Nourished by faith and patience –
> neither of which is plain to see;
> *Travelling the road to freedom,*
> *Who wants to travel the road with me?*
>
> Travelling the road to freedom,
> Who wants to travel the road with me?
> Tipping the scales of justice,
> Setting both minds and captives free;
> Suffering and yet forgiving
> Even when my friends most disagree:
> *Travelling the road to freedom,*
> *Who wants to travel the road with me?*
>
> Travelling the road to freedom,
> I am the Way, I'll take you there;

Choose to come on my journey
Or choose to criticize and stare.
Earth's mesmerizing evil
Only a traveller can repair;
Travelling the road to freedom,
I am the Way, I'll take you there.

Wild Goose Worship Group

Prayer

> *Those who walk along the road of selflessness and kind-*
> *ness are brought closer and closer to a holiness that never*
> *isolates them, the holiness of Jesus, the Risen Lord.*

Brother Roger of Taizé

Give God your mind and imagination, your reason and emotions. Ask him to use them to speak to you. Be with Jesus, eager to walk the road of divine righteousness to justice and peace.

Then ask for the gift of concentrated energy. Dismiss the trivial and what hinders and deflects you by enticing you to accept second best. Receive again the vision of God's holiness and love.

Finally ask God to capture your will and harness it in his service. Bring together in yourself humility and confidence that the Spirit of God can put you to work in the world and give glory to the Father.

Prayer

Lord Jesus,
you gave yourself to the Father
in constant humility and self-forgetfulness:

help us to use your courage and patience
in all our service of others;
build up the kingdom of God within us;
that we may know the joy of doing his will
and belong for ever to the community
which longs for the holiness of his creation.

Morning meditation

Begin afresh

Many people enjoy the music of Gustav Mahler, perhaps without knowing he was a conductor as well as a composer. He worked in opera houses conducting other people's music before he began composing his own. Later, when he conducted performances of his symphonies, he would often stop and change the orchestration and sometimes even the notes as the players were rehearsing. He believed nothing in music is immutable, especially the score. He believed each individual musical experience and performance was itself part of the actual process of creativity. For him each performance was unique and unrepeatable. 'And I hope,' he once said to the members of his orchestra, 'you will go on altering my music after I am dead.'

At the beginning of Holy Week, wherever we happen to be and whatever our personal starting point, Mahler's approach is a good way to begin. To observe the rituals and solemnities of the central week in the Christian Year is not just to do something we have done many times before. We do not open the old books of prayer and hymns to perform the actions mechanically and repeat the same thing all over again. The days ahead open up for Jesus' friends and followers an opportunity to create something fresh, something better than before. Each Holy Week is creative in a unique way.

To begin then, strip yourself of 'all that is past', to use the words of the confession; words which are intended to be a radical statement and which will probably come as a surprise if taken as seriously as they are meant to be. On this part of the Christian pilgrimage we no longer need to take anything with us but only to give up 'all that is past' and go ahead, open to what God is doing with us at each moment.

Be with me Lord
as I travel further
along the way of your cross.
Keep me close to the Father in heaven,
open and watchful,
knowing the demand and the comfort of his love.

A second statement of intent for Holy Week may come as even more of a surprise. We should not concentrate so much on the historical events of the Passion of Christ that we collapse under them.

One year at the beginning of Lent I heard on the radio a very impressive performance of Bach's *St John Passion*. It was sung by the present choir of Bach's church in Leipzig, the Thomaskirche, during a tour of England – their first tour abroad after the collapse of the eastern bloc. Up until that time the choir had been virtually imprisoned, locked into East Germany. At last they were free and able to sing wherever they liked. Their Director of Music, Professor Georg Biller, was interviewed during the interval of the concert. He spoke in German, and was asked whether the privilege of being in Bach's shoes was an impossible role for anyone to undertake. He said – deliberately he did not dwell on the heritage – he had to put it out of his mind, otherwise he could not even begin to do his job. He wouldn't be able to put his hands to the keyboard or raise his arms to conduct soloists or the choir. 'Instead,' he said, 'I try to do what I have to do with the same integrity and inspiration which Bach had; and then,' he added (with the best comment of all), 'I hope when we meet in heaven he will not say to me, "Get lost!" '

Followers of Jesus need the same balance between past and present and between Master and disciple in Holy Week. We do indeed follow paths along some of which Jesus has passed before and all of which he knows. But he has carried his cross, and now he promises to be present and share his strength with us as we carry our own.

The four Gospels have been called Passion Narratives with extended introductions, but significantly they too strip away much of the past in order to release the power of the Good News in the present. Unlike much Christian art and devotion of the late Middle Ages (especially the fifteenth century), the Gospels and the other New Testament writings do not dwell on the terrible details of Jesus' suffering. They do not over-play the horrors of what happened to his body, mind and spirit. Ruthlessly and for good reason they cut back the details of the narrative to a minimum. Strange as it may sound, they underplay what might have been said, so that disciples, in taking up their own cross, are not crushed under the weight of the facts and memory of Jesus' cross.

During any Holy Week each person will almost certainly be carrying both an exterior and an interior cross; the cross of some terrible crisis or crises in world events and a personal, secret cross known only to each person in his or her own heart. Both are threatening. Either can destroy our faith and our confidence in the gospel, our hope in the divine sovereignty. In the process of carrying our burden, any victory we are given over inner chaos and disintegration may well be less than complete. Yet if we allow God to do the judging and saving, then that victory, however small, will be *permanent* – because it will be part of the victory of Jesus, which is itself part of God's own victory over evil.

> Be with me, Lord Jesus.
> Help me to carry my cross:
> both outer and inner pain and suffering.
> Help me to use your strength,
> which you won for me
> by your own journey through Jerusalem,
> and Gethsemane,
> to Calvary.

Evening meditation

Doing without

In Holy Week we should try very hard to come close to God, which sounds and is an obvious thing to say. But it is less obvious but equally important that we should try hard to come as close as possible to the world; a strategy which may not come to the top of our priorities, unless we work at it.

All too often the world is something we fear and prefer to walk away from rather than seek out. To be close to God and close to the world is frightening; not only because of the demands of God's holiness and because of the tragedies of humanity, but also because such closeness inevitably sets up a distance between us and the Church. At Calvary, in a sense, there was God and there was the world and there was no Church. If you like, on the first Good Friday the Church had not yet been invented, it was not yet in being.

Somehow the Church can take us away from God just as it can take us away from the world, especially if we misunderstand its role. One of the most penetrating questions which faces anyone who is really 'at the cross' is, can we do without the Church? Can we do without its securities and companionship? Can we find our faith just by being with God and by being with the world? If we can, then in that moment of what may well be a fearful emptiness there is a real chance that the Church as it truly should be – the crucified and risen Body of Christ – will come into existence.

Dietrich Bonhoeffer was executed by the Nazis on 9 April 1945, a Monday. In prison he had developed his idea of 'religionless Christianity'. It is difficult and probably impossible entirely to know what he meant by this phrase, but I believe at least he meant what has to be faced at every Calvary. In prison he knew God and the full force of the world, and between them he found what it is like to do without the Church.

Yet on the day before he died, the last Sunday of his life, the friends who were with him noticed how little this deprivation had taken him away from either prayer or God. They remembered how he spoke 'in a manner which reached the hearts of all, finding just the right words to express the spirit of our imprisonment, and the thoughts and resolutions it had brought'. Being close to God while being confronted by the world, with its terror and cruelty, proved to be enough.

Be with me, Lord Jesus,
and help me to draw closer and closer to God.
Help me to put away all my sin.
With all your love and self-giving power
pronounce for me the divine forgiveness.
Make me strong to take all that comes at me
from the world around:
its beauty and pain,
its glory and tragedy,
its truth and deceit.

Monday in Holy Week

Surrounding darkness

Morning meditation

Watching with Christ

> When they reached a place called Gethsemane, Jesus said to his disciples, 'Sit here while I pray.' And he took Peter and James and John with him. Horror and dismay came over him, and he said to them, 'My heart is ready to break with grief; stop here, and stay awake.'
>
> Mark 14:32–34

Two German friends from Halle, the birthplace of George Frederick Handel, stayed with me during their first visit to England. Monika and Christoph could only be away from work for five days (they are both Lutheran pastors), and allowing for travelling, that meant they only had three days with me. A trip had been arranged for them by another friend, and the second day would be spent seeing Hereford. Where else would they like to go? Immediately they knew – they wanted to go to Coventry, to see the world-famous cross of nails.

When they came back, they brought with them a cathedral guidebook in which I found these memorable words: 'The world is marked by numberless places where the wounds of history still bleed, where the brooding memory of hurt and hatred lingers.'

Every year, every month, almost every week, the list of places in the world where there is tragedy and sorrow grows longer. The list never ends and is never finally up to date. We can call to mind so many places. Dunblane has now become such a place, where the memory of hurt will linger for a long time – indeed, perhaps for ever. Believe it or not, day-trips can be booked to Auschwitz in Poland and to Dachau near Munich – both places where the wounds of history still bleed. I deliberately visited the village of Oradour sur Glane near Limoges in France to see the twisted metal of the children's prams and the men's bicycles and the women's sewing machines which have been left in the burnt-out homes as a memorial to the day, over fifty years ago now, when following the D-Day landings, the SS took reprisals and mercilessly destroyed the entire village.

All these places, where the brooding memory of hurt and hatred lingers, circle around another place which is burnt into our minds and which will also never be forgotten:

> There is a green hill far away,
> without a city wall,
> where the dear Lord was crucified,
> who died to save us all.

Jesus was executed with a death sentence probably no more cruel and pitiless than many others meted out to those who have suffered injustice and violence in human history, and yet it is to his cross that people continue to bring their suffering and grief, to see whether at least some meaning can be found within so much meaninglessness. People continually gather before the cross to watch and wait and pray.

Archbishop Michael Ramsey used to describe the cross as 'a shaft of light in the world's darkness' – not an answer to the problem of evil, but a shaft of light which begins to illuminate it. The questions which the cross raises – probing, disturbing and rebuilding faith – are much more significant than the faltering and inadequate so-called 'answers' which have sometimes been offered. Look again at God and his world, with its horror and pain, alongside that shaft of light to find out how much meaning and truth it sheds on both.

God, the Father of all,
whose own dear Son
was held in the grip of evil
and crushed by its weight and pain:
be with me
while with tears
and straining mind and breaking heart
I look within the darkness
for you and your loving purposes.

Evening meditation

Tragedy

'What shall I do with the man you call king of the Jews?' They shouted back, 'Crucify him!' 'Why, what harm has he done?' Pilate asked; but they shouted all the louder, 'Crucify him!' So Pilate, in his desire to satisfy the mob, released Barabbas to them; and he had Jesus flogged and handed him over to be crucified.

Mark 15:12–15

The hymns and rites for Holy Week are solemn and stark, all leading to Friday, when the whole day feels hard and cold, blank and empty. Yet Christians will call next Friday *a Good day* (though we should not do so too easily or without proper care and thought) because there is something else happening within Jesus' death as well as the dramatic events at Pilate's palace and Calvary; something deeper than anything a TV reporter's camera team could have recorded. On the surface all we see is yet more cruelty and dehumanization, but Christians call this the climax of 'the tale of the loving purposes of God'.

At times the truth remains obscure, hidden, secret; yet at other times suddenly it can become extraordinarily clear and straightforward, rather like the sun which floods a dark room. So much is seen which previously had been missed. The hill of Calvary is not a place of ifs and buts, of perhaps and maybe. Cutting through human confusions, it offers facts together with definite and clear-cut possibilities and new perspectives. Afterwards the clouds may well return and the light will recede, but the glimpses of truth remain for us to grasp and hold.

A particular kind of insight is needed to enable anyone to interpret the narrative of Jesus' suffering and death in such a way and to give to the cross this positive and powerful interpretation. Jesus said, 'I, if I be lifted up, will draw all people to myself' (John 12:32). Human beings made in the image of God are meant to be his co-workers and companions. Instead, too often they either never identify their vocation or they fall away from such a high and demanding destiny.

Think of two children playing with a box of bricks. One, putting them together carefully, is building a wall or a house. While the other almost as fast is taking them down, pulling them out of their place and throwing them about haphazardly, all too rapidly destroying what is being so painstakingly built.

The conflict between God's purposes and our wilful, ill-informed behaviour is the source of the tragedy of Good Friday. See God, who is the creative, purposeful energy at work within the world, pulling things together, putting them in order, establishing the scaffolding to build unity, coherence, peace. Then see ourselves, bending our energies in many directions which take his work apart. We just don't realize what God is doing and nor do we realize exactly what we are doing. Ignorant sometimes because of wickedness and deliberate sin, and sometimes through stupidity and blindness. A prophet puts into words, clearly and emphatically, the depth of God's knowledge of his people and their failure: 'Your ways are not my ways, and your thoughts are not my thoughts' (Isa. 55:8). Yet God never stops loving all he is making and all he has made.

We are faced with an ultimate question: Is the cross – an obscene object devised by twisted minds for extreme torture – the place of the world's salvation or is it the final empty folly of all time? Such an awesome place of choosing acts like a magnet and draws every human being at some time or other to it and holds them until a decision is taken.

I noticed another quotation in the guidebook to Coventry Cathedral which reads, 'At the moment of choice between one way or the other, in C. S. Lewis's words, "the angels of God hold their breath to see which way we will choose to go." '

Originally the definition of tragedy was *a falling away from God* and comedy was *a coming back to God*, which provides another thread of meaning hidden within the events of Jesus' death. This is the story of our falling away from God and our rescue, his bringing us back to him.

There was a day in Jesus' ministry when Peter rashly, and

almost speaking out of turn, but with unique insight, spoke the truth about Jesus and his messiahship (Matt. 16:15–17). Jesus' reply is worth remembering when we are looking for meaning in his suffering and death: 'Flesh and blood hath not revealed this to you, but my Father which is in heaven.' Being close to both the cross of Jesus and to our own cross, whatever form it takes, we need to look for something which speaks of God rather than of flesh and blood and which indeed comes to us from God and is revealed by the Father rather than unravelled from within ourselves. The insight we seek in Holy Week is God-given, part of his saving grace, a sign of his presence with us in every aspect of our living, and is the reality of his loving.

Lord Jesus Christ,
you promised to pray to your heavenly Father
for each one of us:
pray with me now
that I may receive from him
a new vision of truth,
a new understanding of his purposes
and a new depth of love.

Tuesday in Holy Week

Standing before God

Morning meditation

Forgiveness

> There were two others with Jesus, criminals who were being led away to execution; and when they reached the place called The Skull, they crucified him there, and the criminals with him, one on his right and the other on his left. Jesus said, 'Father, forgive them; they do not know what they are doing.'
>
> Luke 23:32–34

The cross of nails at Coventry has been placed in front of the words 'Father forgive' which have been carved into the ruined walls of the old cathedral. Forgiveness is the way to cut through the vicious circles of human violence and pain. People have discovered it for themselves at Coventry and at Dresden, at Enniskillen and Warrington, and the observers and witnesses of such forgiveness are awestruck at the amazing sight. How can those who have been injured or bereaved, engulfed in tragedy, yet be willing to forgive? After tragedy, they turn to forgiveness as the one remaining opportunity for hope and renewal.

From the sidelines others marvel and wonder if they could ever do the same, but, to be fair, most people have some interior knowledge and experience of the hard and demanding road of forgiveness. For example, Michael and Elaine Counsell whose little boy was killed by a hit-and-run driver were able to forgive him. Not everyone wants to forgive. Some find it impossible. Ruth Fuller, elderly, sharply intelligent and sad, whose son was killed in a knife fight with a thug, said, 'Never.' Tim Parry's father said he would work for peace in Ireland but he could never forgive those who killed his son. That all makes sense and we understand – more with our hearts than with our heads. We also know though that those who cannot eventually find the way to forgive remain cut off from the sources of healing, and stay dangerously close to the forces of evil which have already touched them so savagely.

Jesus gave more than an example when he prayed for forgiveness for those who had brought him to the cross. At the same time he revealed the cost and the method of divine forgiveness in every situation. 'For their sake I consecrate myself,' he said (John 17:19), and throughout his ministry Jesus lived what he believed. Going to the cross became part of his total self-consecration to God and his task as God's servant, commissioned and equipped to bring in the kingdom. For those who identify with Jesus and at least attempt to follow him, a concentrated consecration of self for the sake of others always enables those who are searching for the way to forgiveness to find it.

When Jesus prayed for those who crucified him he said they did not know what they were doing. Often what we think we know is ignorance in disguise, and usually we are too frightened to admit how little knowledge we have. We should be honest and face human ignorance, which remains extensive in spite of the great harvest of modern research and enquiry. On the other hand, we should never allow what we don't know to threaten or destroy what we do know. While he was Bishop of Birmingham, Leonard Wilson, who suffered in Singapore during the Second World War, used to say that the older he grew the less he was sure of – but, he always added, at the same time he became more and more convinced of the few things which remained certain to him.

To the end, Jesus remained convinced that whatever else was happening, the kingdom of his Father was being established through him, even though sometimes it all seemed blurred and a long way off. He taught that the way to this kingdom was straight and the entrance gate narrow, a conviction which brought him to the thin and painful strips of wood which made the cross and proved to be the narrow way into the kingdom of heaven for all believers. Nor is the source of such reliable and costly knowledge entirely hidden. 'The fear of the Lord, that is wisdom; to depart from evil is understanding' (Prov. 3:7).

Part of the purpose of keeping Holy Week is to detach ourselves from the power of evil and to attach ourselves more firmly to all that is good. 'Deeply were we stained,' we sing in one the Christmas carols. 'It was while we were yet sinners that Christ died for us' (Rom. 5:8), says St Paul. We want to belong to the forgiving, healing power within the world, which we identify and name God. To come as close as we can to that power we need to know how much we ourselves have been forgiven and how much remains in us to be forgiven.

Face to face with God, especially through and during the death of Jesus, we encounter the miracle of divine, unconditional forgiveness and unending love. Receiving God's forgiveness ourselves make us eager to forgive. Every time this inner miracle of forgiveness happens to us, God's love is at work and flowing. Then the experience of being forgiven becomes the everlasting spring which feeds all the wells of forgiveness in the universe, whether in ourselves or in others.

There was a scaffold in a courtyard of our prison in Dachau concentration camp. I used to look at it every day to receive its sermon. I had to pray a good many times because of it. It was not that I was afraid of being hanged on its scaffold one fine morning – one gets used even to this prospect as we all get used to the idea of having to die one day. No, what scared me was what I would do at the crucial moment. Would I cry out with my last breath: 'You are making me die like a criminal but you Nazis are the real criminals. There's a God in heaven and one day He'll prove it to you.'

If Christ had died like that, there would never have been a Gospel of the cross. No forgiveness, no salvation, no hope. There would have been no reconciliation on God's part; the Son of Man would never have been the Son of God. There would have been no new humanity bearing the very image of God Himself. He would simply have been in the presence of just another specimen of our race, this inhuman human race.

If I were to die like that, even in the name of Christ, I would die an unbeliever. Not believing that the prayer of Jesus prayed on the cross was meant for me too. For none of us can live by the grace of God, none of us can be reconciled with Him, unless by that same token at the same time we offer mercy and forgiveness to our fellow human beings. And, without the grace of God, we are of no greater worth than anyone else, even an SS man!

Martin Niemöller
(from *Against Torture*)

Lord Jesus, you pray for forgiveness
for all those who betray and kill you:
Lord Jesus, you open the Father's heart of love
and we too are forgiven
whenever we are the cause of more hurt and pain.
Lord Jesus, help us never to withhold from others
the forgiveness
we have so freely and undeservedly received.

Evening meditation

Presence

One of the criminals who hung there with Jesus taunted
him: 'Are not you the Messiah? Save yourself, and us.' But
the other rebuked him: 'Have you no fear of God? You are
under the same sentence as he. For us it is plain justice; we
are paying the price for our misdeeds; but this man has
done nothing wrong.' And he said, 'Jesus, remember me
when you come to your throne.' Jesus answered, 'I tell you
this: today you shall be with me in Paradise.'

Luke 23:39–43

Dr Sheila Cassidy was interrogated and tortured by the secret
police in Chile in 1975. Somehow within the torture she knew
the presence of God. In her own words:

If you could imagine a situation where somebody you
know was actually a bystander at something horrible
happening to you, not intervening, knowing they were
there but not achieving any comfort from the fact that the
person was there. I've no idea why God wasn't intervening.
History shows that God doesn't intervene in a lot of

things. There's nothing special about me! The curious thing is that all that time that it was happening I knew God loved me. Don't ask me how ... it was a very curious clinical thing like God being present in an operating theatre.[3]

The thief hanging beside Jesus also knew instinctively that God was there, present in a particular and precise though indefinable way. He turned to Jesus not with complaint, nor joining in with the abuse of others, but with an acknowledgement of Jesus' mission to bring in God's kingdom. Simply and directly, which some would dismiss as naive, he asked to be remembered as one who recognized and accepted the divine rule. Experiencing the presence of God with such power always brings the kingdom very close, only a step away.

Before he left his disciples Jesus told them he was going to the Father, and he also told them the purpose of his journey to God: in order that 'where I am you may be also' (John 14:3). The thief being executed with Jesus would not only be remembered but would also find himself in the presence of God, with Jesus himself there with him too. 'Today,' says Jesus, 'you shall be with me in paradise.' At Ascensiontide we recall this promise of Jesus and turn it into prayer, when we use the old collect and pray that 'we may be exalted to the same place whither our Saviour Christ has gone before'.

One of the purposes of Jesus' death and exaltation is to establish an unbroken presence between God and ourselves which will exist and endure both in this world and the next. We aspire to God's kingdom in order to be with Jesus forever, and he promises to be with us now in this life and in whatever life lies ahead. 'Lo, I am with you always until the end of time' (Matt. 28:20). From now on we are to be with him, wherever he is: and he is with us, wherever we are.

To watch with Christ at Calvary can be a powerful sign of

our willingness to be with Jesus, occupying the same space, as we say; being in the same 'room' as he is. We are there with him as both guest and friend. We have been invited – ' "Take up thy cross," the Saviour said, "if thou wouldst my disciple be" ' – as friends – 'No longer do I call you servants for the servant does not know what his master is doing; but I have called you friends, for all that I have heard from my Father I have made known to you' (John 15:15).

We are present with Jesus with a purpose. Occupying the same space with him, we must share in his work. 'In very truth I tell you, he who has faith in me will do what I am doing; and he will do greater things still because I am going to the Father' (John 14:12). Jesus keeps neither himself nor his task to himself. He shares both with his disciples as together we move closer to his cross and with more determination shoulder our own.

Friends always want to be together, for friendship is mutual desire and nothing enriches friendship so much as sharing a common task. 'We'll build the garage together,' they promise each other. 'I'll get a friend to help me,' we've all said from time to time. 'Let's work in the garden tomorrow,' one promises another. Those who play together in a string quartet or a brass band, or sing in a madrigal group usually become friends simply by working together at a common task. To be a team player in any game or recreation offers a bonus of comradeship and fellowship.

And there is a blessing. Being at one with Jesus, being companions with him, knowing his presence and sharing his work, sets our troubled hearts at rest. We are among those who have been given to him by the Father and for whom he constantly prays (John 17:6–10).

Just after Christmas one year, I went to visit the Benedictine monastery at St Wandrille near Rouen in the

Seine valley. Their buildings were destroyed in the French revolution but in 1969 a community of monks returned to the old site. Now they give a leaflet to every visitor to explain the purpose of their community. It says they are there 'to be present to God and present to the neighbour', a phrase which strips away a good deal of the guff and fluff about discipleship and witness and sums up with simplicity exactly the character and purpose of discipleship.

We follow Jesus and stand by his cross not to convert the world or to change it into God's kingdom – that process of conversion and growth is the divine activity which goes on constantly whether we realize it or not, and despite us as well as occasionally because of us. Our task is to be present to God and present to neighbour, avoiding a pious, self-conscious, self-indulgent, bothersome, do-goodery posturing (all the things people understandably dislike about Christians), but being there in a simple, direct way. Standing with God and neighbour to be available and to be used by both.

If we are lethargic and slow to be with Jesus, then the energy and the movement will be all God's. Like the father of the Prodigal Son (Luke 15:11–32), in the cross of Jesus, at the cost of total self-giving, God moves towards us with words of welcome and friendship and forgiveness. His purpose in creating us is being brought to fulfilment and completion through the cross: that 'he may be in us and we in him', enjoying him for ever.

Lord Jesus,
you promised the thief
hanging beside you
that he would know the presence of God:
be with us now

where we are,
so that we may also be with you
in the glory of your Father's kingdom.

Wednesday in Holy Week

Facing the end

Morning meditation

Relationship

Meanwhile near the cross where Jesus hung stood his mother, with her sister, Mary wife of Clopas, and Mary of Magdala. Jesus saw his mother, with the disciple whom he loved standing beside her. He said to her, 'Mother, there is your son'; and to the disciple, 'There is your mother'; and from that moment the disciple took her into his home.

John 19:25–27

'Like father, like son,' we say, sometimes in praise, more often to blame; or indeed, 'Like mother, like daughter.' Behind such remarks is the realization of how interdependent we are with each other and how much we shape one another's lives. We are what we are not only because of our personal inner life (although that is very telling) but also because of who and what others are like around us. They influence us in ways both known and unknown. They are involved in creating us just as sometimes they nearly destroy us. We grow within the family and against it. We are by turns dependent and independent, each mood equally necessary when its time comes.

The same is true with friends and colleagues. They can determine to a great extent where we succeed and where we fail. I shall never forget when this lesson came home to me in all its power and mystery. It was while I was a parish priest and we were going through a particularly difficult time in the parish. Like any priest, I was involved up to the hilt in the distress and the concern, but I had to learn that I was lost in it all in a destructive rather than a healing way. One member of the PCC was very supportive and encouraging, but in the end she could bear it no longer. She faced me and said, 'Have you any idea what you are doing to us?' The truth was no, I hadn't – I had only considered what they were doing to one another, without realizing how deeply involved I was too. We are bound one with another, bound 'in the bundle of the living' (1 Sam. 25:29), for better and for worse.

The two relationship words *family* and *community* are basic for the gospel, and we start to hear them when we relate to God and hear his Good News. Or, rather (because it is always God who takes the first step) when he enables us to accept that he is already relating to us. He is the initiator, the one who is pro-active, to use the current, fashionable phrase. The cross is a sign and demonstration of the extent of God's love for us. This divine loving is the origin of all our relating and all our opportunities for growth and development within our relationships. The cross stands at the heart of the New Testament writings and at the heart of Christian history, because it declares God's love for us once and for all, and sets human beings free to do the kind of loving which is truly creative, fulfilling and lasting.

God's love is both strong and tender, both fierce and kind, both demanding and satisfying. Probably it is wrong to say that God's loving is the feminine in God. God's love for his creation could just as easily be the most male aspect of the divine love. Many have become very confused about what it is to be male and female, and they muddle it all up with gender and sexuality. Self-giving love and tenderness, of which God's love is the pattern, is as much a masculine characteristic and need as it is feminine. God wants us to recover loving in all its aspects: loving which in every respect is as much for men as it is for women. For in God there is neither male nor female but a unity of being (Gal. 3:28).

Another image of relationship which Jesus uses is the vine and the branches. Notice two things: they are not attached to each other by association but through growth, and the purpose of the attachment of the branch to the vine is that it may bear fruit and *go on bearing fruit* (John 15:16). When we belong, we are not free to roam, nor are we meant to. Belonging to a community or in a particular relationship with another properly has its limitations. We have to be plugged in, as it were, and stay that way if we are to find fulfilment and harvest, if we are to abide in God and he is to be in us. Stability is the second of the three vows which hold together the Benedictine Order. The members promise to belong *and to go on belonging* to God and to their community: a sign that they understand how the vine and the branches are one and simply do not exist without each other.

Jesus asked Mary to accept John as her son and he asked John to take her as his mother because he knew the extent to which they would need each other in the future. Knowing their human need, he gave them to each other in a unique way, creating a new family and a new community. Slowly we are beginning to discover how family and community articulate and satisfy something which human beings need for their own personal development and well-being as well as something which benefits and structures society. From within the cross Jesus creates a new family and the first Christian community through his own continual loving, which springs from the mutual love he has with his Father.

We don't know whether Mary and John found their new relationship easy or whether they had to work at it. Constantly we hear of failed relationships, broken relationships, relationships betrayed, underlining that every relationship is always costly. Human failure and frailty push us to seek healing and wholeness, and the Christian claim that all human relationships need to be brought to God to allow his love to sustain them and make them fruitful is more relevant than ever nowadays.

Yet the new relationship created by Jesus was more something done to Mary and John that something done by them. Often that is how it happens because so much inner growth in the spiritual life comes from pressures outside ourselves to which we are pushed to respond. Rarely can we generate all that much from within ourselves. We have to be more open to receive the rest, usually given from sources over which we have no control. At the cross God in Christ comes to us and places us at the point where new life and hope are given. Because we shall never be able to save ourselves, there is no other way.

Lord Jesus,
you gave Mary and John
into each other's love and carefulness:
help us to receive with joy and acceptance
those to whom we have been given.
May we know the relationship we have with God,
which you are creating by your dying and rising;
then enrich our lives with the love and fulfilment
which are in God,
always drawing us forward into him.

Evening meditation

Void

> From midday a darkness fell over the whole land, which
> lasted until three in the afternoon; and about three Jesus
> cried aloud, '*Eli, Eli, lema sabachthani?*' which means, 'My
> God, my God, why hast thou forsaken me?' Some of the
> bystanders, on hearing this said, 'He is calling Elijah.' One
> of them ran at once and fetched a sponge, which he soaked
> in sour wine, and held it to his lips on the end of a cane.
> But the others said, 'Let us see if Elijah will come to save
> him.'
>
> Matthew 27:45–49

A lady in Suffolk was about to celebrate her eightieth
birthday. She wrote to her family and friends begging them
not to give her things. 'I'm trying to give things away, not
keep them,' she said. She didn't need things any more. Quite
properly she was considering her mortality and preparing for
a holy and happy death, for which, from time to time, we too
should pray, whatever age we are.

As we approach death there is a growing sense of with-
drawing. The circles surrounding us begin to collapse and
narrow. All the circumstances which normally hold us
together in one piece and give our lives meaning and significance fall away. Essentially to die is to be alone, to face a void.

This void is more than a desert emptiness and becomes
total isolation. No one can be truly with us, however much
they sympathize or stay with us and stand alongside us at the
time. Each person's death is unique, one-off, unrepeatable.
We are more than grateful for those who do stay with us to
the end, but we cannot expect them to know the particular
kind of fear being faced from the inside, precisely because

this is the one place they cannot yet have visited for themselves. Frequently people tell us how few actually fear being dead, though they say they fear the terrible trouble of getting there, which includes passing through this void and becoming more and more isolated and alone.

Gerald Priestland once described the numbness inflicted by intense pain and suffering; in his case clinical depression. He urged those wanting to help to resist the temptation to say such things as 'I know how you're feeling' or to offer pious remarks about Jesus' suffering on the cross. At the time, he said, such words simply do not help. Perhaps the same applies to dying. Perhaps all comfort then is for the time being cold comfort.

Yet there is something remaining which we can hold on to. The experience of facing death is a Highest Common Factor possessed by all human beings. Like birth, it is the one thing everyone must experience. The human race is a community of suffering and also a community of those who are (or should be) outraged by the blankness of death, and who always face it uniquely, once and for all, and therefore – inevitably at the time – entirely alone.

As Jesus faces the ultimateness and loneliness of his death, there is a preliminary void into which he enters. He endures the loss of his sense of God. No one will ever know whether he expected this to happen or not, or whether he had in any way prepared himself for it. To feel forsaken by God is the ultimate affliction. Just to glimpse it a little, imagine an intrusive modern reporter pushing his way into the garden of Gethsemane or through the crowds of Calvary and asking Jesus the appalling interviewer's question, 'How are you feeling at this moment?' The ludicrousness, absurdity, insensitivity and indeed cruelty of such an approach may put us in touch with something of the void into which Jesus entered.

Some have said the collapse of all contact with God, at some time or another, is part of what it means to be human. The irony is that, according to the Jewish faith, one of God's promises to his people is always to be there, to be present in affliction. Every Jew was taught that God keeps his promises for ever. But in view of the divine promise and faithfulness which was the heart of Jesus' faith in his Father's love, would it be better to ask if what is happening is not so much that God is absent and withdrawn but that the signs of God's presence are shifting and changing through such agony? Perhaps what is being learned is a new and larger vocabulary of how we can speak of God being with us. If so, in the void we find more of the words we must use when we say, too easily at times, that God is with us and all his people.

Recently I have spent time with a mother of deep faith who has had to live through the death of her son in particularly painful circumstances. The only thing I know is that all the old words of her faith lost their meaning. They were lost not because they were false or misleading but because they had become a cauldron in which new words of faith were being forged and shaped. It became a time when silence was essential, and we both needed to avoid chatter and even cosy, comfy, spiritual counsel. Instead we stayed together and faced in silence the fearful void of human mortality, silent and searching for new words of faith.

Jesus goes through the same experience. In spite of his deep and lasting intimacy with his Father, he passes the same way as the rest of the human race in particularly agonizing circumstances. On the cross he feels cut off and forsaken. Here for him is the void into which we shall all not only stare but actually eventually enter. If there is any meaning to be found in death, it can only come out of such total collapse.

Once the circles have closed in and nothing more than a

pinpoint is left, we have God's promise that then something new does come. The circles enlarge again, widen and reach out to include not just this world but the whole of reality – all that we have been and all that is to come. We could dismiss the possibility as only a promise, but its strength and credibility come from the One who is making it. Face to face with such ultimateness that is what matters – and whether or not we have come to know and trust him as 'a faithful Creator' (1 Pet. 4:19).

Edith Evans was once asked how she remembered all her long speeches, especially the ones in Shakespeare and George Bernard Shaw. She gave an unforgettable answer. 'Think of the last line,' she said, 'and draw it towards you.' All Christians can adopt the same discipline and, like every monk and nun who is required to face death daily, draw the end towards us – not as a rehearsal, but as part of entering the fearful void which in the end cannot be (literally) a-voided, but through which, because of what happened to Jesus, we believe confidently we shall pass.

> Lord Jesus,
> we cannot know the depth of your falling away
> from your Father's love;
> how it cut your mind and spirit into pieces
> and shattered your very being:
> but as you passed through death
> and learned new thoughts and words
> of hope and trust,
> be with us when we make the same journey,
> that we may come to live by your faith.

Thursday in Holy Week

Giving in obedience

Morning meditation

Need

> Jesus, aware that all had now come to its appointed end, said in fulfilment of Scripture, 'I thirst.' A jar stood there full of sour wine; so they soaked a sponge with the wine, fixed it on a javelin, and held it up to his lips.
>
> John 19:28–29

Most clergy houses get used to the regular visits of a variety of men and, more occasionally, women of the road. They come in need – of money mostly, but sometimes seeking food and clothing, and sometimes wanting companionship, a chat, a sign of recognition and acceptance. Frances Young, a Methodist minister, has her fair share at her home in Birmingham. She became quite fond of one of them – a regular Irish tramp who, when he left, often used to say, 'I always say a prayer for you, lady.' That, as she says, reminds us of how much the rich need the poor rather than the other way round.[4] Even those who are reasonably secure need prayer, and there are no restrictions about where it can come from.

Such an idea of mutuality, whatever our condition and

whatever our individual need, goes right back to the early Church, which was a community where all acknowledged that they were in need of something. There was no division between the haves and the have-nots, although there were certainly some among them who had more than others. The same concept obviously lies behind the Welfare State, the nineteenth-century poor acts and the ladies of charity who preceded them. Many say they find modern charity patronizing. Whether this is special pleading or not, it does suggest that those in need should never have their dignity discarded. It would be better if we could re-establish the long-standing Christian concept of community as all who live together with shared needs. A Christian is one beggar telling another beggar where to find bread.

In the world today we are confronted by vast need, and social commentators warn us of compassion fatigue. Perhaps Jesus can save us a little from this too. He was one who looked for a cup of water, and he was the one who had already said in a parable, 'inasmuch as you do it to one of the least of these little ones you do it to me' (Matt. 25:40). Jesus' cry for water could easily be submerged in the desperation of the millions undergoing agonizing thirst and hunger, but his cry for help from the cross was answered. Thankfully someone had enough humanity and compassion to respond and leave the world an example in the most direct and immediate way of how to meet another's cry for help.

Bishop John V. Taylor sees part of the future for Christians, especially as they confront the division between rich and poor, like this:

> Hitherto the European and North American churches' comprehension of the poverty of fellow Christians in the southern continents has consisted mainly of news

coverage, imagination and generosity. It has perforce been a relationship of 'we' and 'they'. But as communication technology makes immediate personal contact across the world accessible to far more people, as business enter-prises, even on the smaller scale, become transnational, as Christian leaders from the economically deprived coun-tries play a frequent and prominent part in international synods and assemblies of the churches, as the twinning of dioceses and congregations of the North with the South grows more personalised, and 'partnership' consultations become more mutually outspoken, and as the issue of poverty in the richer nations gets more perceptibly similar in structure if not in degree to that in the southern conti-nents, sympathy will inevitably give place to solidarity, and it will be normal for Christian self-awareness to include all in a common 'us'. Then intercession will tend to fade into petition: 'Have mercy on us all' rather than 'help them'.[5]

All human need is a sign of the total dependence on God of the whole human race and, just as important though not so often noticed, it is also a sign of his equally total self-giving. 'Blessed are those who hunger and thirst for righteousness, for they shall be satisfied,' Jesus promised (Matt. 5:6).

Even though, as his life drained away, all Jesus received was a tiny token of that promised fulfilment – a sponge dipped in vinegar – in the fierce agony of human need he knew the coming of his Father's kingdom of righteousness.

Jesus used another image as a way of speaking of his death: a full chalice of wine, drunk to the dregs. With his thirst assuaged a little, he still has to drink to the last drop the cup of his Father's will. His ordeal is not yet over, and he goes further into suffering.

We may not manage to achieve much to ameliorate the

terrible need of the world, and what we struggle to do will appear to be little more than the sponge of vinegar offered to Jesus, but that must not discourage us or deflect us from going ahead in the demanding and never-ending task of serving others. Archbishop Michael Ramsey always pictured the Christian pilgrimage as a single movement towards God in adoration and into the darkness of the world in service.[6] The two cannot be separated, and we cannot have one without the other. In an unexpected and often overlooked way, those in need come to us offering a precious gift – the opportunity to be drawn closer to God and to go deeper into our knowledge of him through serving those whom he gives us in their need.

> Lord Jesus,
> now among the hungry and thirsty,
> on the cross in your agony
> you received a token of compassion
> from one who stood nearby:
> help us always to be among those who
> hear the desperate cries of anguish
> from your brothers and sisters,
> and make us ready, eager and able to help.

Evening meditation

Obedience

Humble yourselves therefore under the mighty hand of God, that in due time he may exalt you. Cast all your anxieties on him, for he cares about you. Be sober, be watchful. Your adversary the devil prowls around like a roaring lion, seeking someone to devour. Resist him, firm in your faith, knowing that the same experience of suffering is required of your brotherhood throughout the world. And after you have suffered a little while, the God of all grace, who has called you to his eternal glory in Christ, will himself restore, establish, and strengthen you.

1 Peter 5:6–10

Outside the Sebalduskirche in Nuremberg there is a large and famous sculpture of Jesus at prayer in Gethsemane. When I first saw it I thought the subject was inappropriate for the crowds constantly passing by and at odds with such a public place. But perhaps the message is that in spite of our indifference, Jesus, at the cost of his own self-giving and sacrifice, is for ever winning salvation and a harvest of grace for the whole human race. Whether we will attend and respond or not, the work of God's redeeming love never ceases.

An ancient custom for Christians is to observe a vigil of prayer on the night before Good Friday. In heart and mind we follow Jesus to a quiet place and face in ourselves something of the agonizing struggle between self-will and God's will. Maybe it is not too difficult to know what is self-will, and usually others are very ready to tell us if this is where we are blind, but often exactly what is God's will remains extremely unclear. We want to follow, we want obedience, because we know this is the way of salvation, but for whatever reason God's words remain stubbornly muffled and confused to our hearing.

Wrestle with that fact for even a moment, and at least one thing has to be reckoned with. The source of the difficulty will be with us rather than with God. Any confusion or lack of clarity will be because we are hindering ourselves. In Bible language and imagery, we are blind and deaf, held in the grip of some particular sin or sins. In other words, we are being devoured by evil, which St Peter calls the devil and to whom picturesquely he gives the characteristics of a hungry beast of prey. Evil in any of its guises prevents us from hearing God clearly. Unless and until we acknowledge the fact and make it a starting point in our discipleship, we cannot make much sense of anything else.

Part of the purpose of making confession, whatever form we use, is to restore us to a condition where we can hear God clearly and know his healing and strength. True, God does not always speak just because we talk. He doesn't speak just because we demand answers. But his silences are always creative and never vindictive. If God gives us space and withdraws for a time, he does so to help, not to hinder. If he scatters, he will in due time gather again. Like the disciples with Jesus in the garden, we must watch and wait and pray. Then, if we can, we will want to go further and make our waiting upon God an offering of obedience. 'Yet not my will but thine be done' (Luke 22:42).

Sadly, obedience sounds a dry, heavy, unattractive word. It doesn't immediately appeal and describe enrichment, development and fulfilment. But in Christian spirituality obedience is the lovely foundation of a generous and flourishing relationship between ourselves and God. The kind of obedience which is based on an exchange of love has been central to the life of Christian people in every age.

When St Benedict wrote about obedience in Chapter 5 of his *Rule*, he taught that it comes from a listening ear, a ready heart, and with the illumination which comes from the gospel. He never asks for or expects unreasoned obedience. Nor does he exclude the personal responsibility of each person to form and follow his or her own conscience. A more contemporary way of expressing Christian obedience has been to use the phrase 'Yes to God'[7] and to see this aspect of Christian spirituality as a continuing process, a series of

Yeses rather than one dramatic statement. Obedience is growth in understanding, in prayer and in living, and is a dynamic response to the care God offers and provides.

Lord Jesus, in the garden,
face to face with evil,
you were utterly alone
and knew agony and desperation.
Take us with you
to the battleground,
but stand beside us
in the silence of our Gethsemane.
Keep us awake
to fight against every kind of sin;
arm us with your strength
to resist the lure of self-desire;
and help us to listen
and to hear the voice of the Father:
so we too may know and do his will.

Good Friday

Going into the dark

Beginning to pray

Lord Jesus,
your body and mind and spirit
were broken and destroyed;
hope went into the grave;
you gave up all
for the sake of each and every person
who is and has been and ever will be;
you followed faithfully and to the end
the vision of your Father's kingdom;
you faced nothingness and emptiness.

Psalm

I stretch out my hands toward you:
my soul yearns for you like a thirsty land.
Be swift to hear me, O Lord, for my spirit fails:
hide not your face from me,
     lest I be like those who go down to the Pit.
O let me hear of your merciful kindness in the morning,
     for my trust is in you:
show me the way I should go,

for you are my hope.
Deliver me from my enemies, O Lord:
for I run to you for shelter.
Teach me to do your will, for you are my God:
let your kindly spirit lead me in an even path.
For your name's sake, O Lord, preserve my life:
and for the sake of your righteousness,

bring me out of trouble.

Psalm 143:6–11

Bible reading

Praise be to the God and Father of our Lord Jesus Christ, the all-merciful Father, the God whose consolation never fails us! He comforts us in all our troubles, so that we in turn may be able to comfort others in any trouble of theirs and to share with them the consolation we ourselves receive from God. As Christ's cup of suffering overflows, and we suffer with him, so also through Christ our consolation overflows. If distress be our lot, it is the price we pay for your consolation, for your salvation; if our lot be consolation, it is to help us bring you comfort, and strength to face with fortitude the same sufferings we now endure. And our hope for you is firmly grounded; for we know that if you have part in the suffering, you have part also in the divine consolation.

2 Corinthians 1:3–7

Song

I believe, although everything
hides you from my faith.
I believe, although everything shouts No! to me.

I believe, although everything may seem to die.
I believe, although I no longer would wish to live,
　　because I have founded my life
　　on a sincere word,
　　on the word of a Friend,
　　on the word of God.

I believe, although I feel alone in pain.
I believe, although I see people hating.
I believe, although I see children weep,
　　because I have learnt with certainty
　　that he comes to meet us
　　in the hardest hours,
　　with his love and his light.
I believe,
　　but increase my faith.

From *Livros de Cantos*

Prayer

Although there may well be shocks and even upheavals in our lives, the Risen Christ is there. He could say to us, 'When you are going through the harshest trials, I am present underneath your despair. And remember I am also in the innermost recesses of your radiant hopes.'

Brother Roger of Taizé

Pray with as much simple directness as you can.
Ask for strength and insight.

Like Jesus, give yourself with quiet confidence into
　　God's hands.
Ask for trust and understanding.

Call into your mind and heart all who are suffering.
Pray by name for those you know who need your prayers.
Look as deeply and persistently as you can
at the struggle between good and evil.
Ask God to take you as you are and place you firmly
and forever within his embracing love and power.

Prayer

Lord Jesus,
in the pain, cruelty and injustice of the cross,
in the full force of its destruction and wickedness,
you faced the terror and horror of evil:
be with us in our darkness
in suffering and sorrow,
in fear and bewilderment,
in emptiness and grief;
hold us close to God
and anchor us to the strength of
his resurrecting love
for ever.

Morning meditation

Achievement

Having received the wine, Jesus said, 'It is accomplished!'
John 19:30

President Nixon labelled a week many can remember as 'the
greatest week since the creation of the world' and an
American writer described it as 'the greatest week since
Christ was born'. The week was in July 1969 when the first

two people from earth walked on the moon. All they found there was a total emptiness and nothingness. Literally they had to take everything with them – including air to breathe. The moon is and was a completely dead environment.

In past centuries, mankind has often dreamed of going to the moon. Among others, a seventeenth-century bishop of Hereford predicted that one day it would happen. All hoped it would mark the dawn of a new era and open a door into an undreamed of future. After twenty-five years, however, there is still nothing much to celebrate about landing on the moon, beyond the amazing technical achievement and a few useful spin-offs. Probably the best thing has been the beautiful pictures of the earth seen from a new perspective, making us gasp just enough to take stock a little and re-examine ourselves as a human race. If we ask if it really was the greatest week since the beginning of the world, probably we shall remain little more than sceptical.

Think of another week and another journey – the week and the events which brought Jesus to his cross. Christians believe these are pivotal events which shape all human history, however long it lasts. An equally vast claim, but is there better substance in making it?

When Jesus reached the hill of Calvary, there was another meeting with emptiness, nothingness, meaninglessness. True, there was a lot more happening within it all than has ever happened on the moon; and true, within the events, a great deal happened which bore much fruit in the future. However, watching Jesus during the final hour of his life, all apparently remains futile – great hopes petering out into the sand, a deep frustration attacking his spirit, a wondering what it could mean and whether it had been worthwhile or not. Jesus could not have put it like this, but we can ask, Was the journey to Calvary as futile as the journey to the moon?

Into this blankness Jesus speaks a word of triumph: 'It is finished.' We have been taught by most scholars and preachers (though not quite all) to hear his cry as a sign of victory rather than defeat. Jesus saw not so much the end of his life as the end and purpose of his work. He had said, 'We must work the works of him who sent me, while it is day; night comes, when no man can work. As long as I am in the world, I am the light of the world' (John 9:4–5). Darkness surrounded and suffocated him in death, but within it all his work was achieved: thanks be to God.

Jesus' work, doing his Father's will, which he said was meat and drink to him (John 4:34), had been of an unusual character. It was work which had to be done from the inside out, as it were. Jesus had preached, 'the kingdom is within you' (Luke 17:21), and by being born himself within human circumstances he became the power inside our humanity which releases it and brings it to fulfilment. There was a famous prisoner during the Second World War named Witold Pilecki, who had himself arrested and sent to a concentration camp deliberately, in order to set others free from the inside.[8]

When evil is rampant, everything mingles in confusion. Good and evil become indistinguishable. Light and darkness, fulfilment and frustration, purpose and sterility – we do not know which is which and we mistake one for the other. Very much the human condition as we know it today and every day, but this is the chaos, like the first chaos, to which God brings order and purpose by his judgement and saving power. On the cross God finishes his work of creation by making the kingdoms of this world into the kingdom of his Son (Rev. 11:15), with a unique act which at one and the same time is creative and redemptive as well.

The journey to Calvary was fruitful because through it Jesus finally brought to birth within this world of time and

space, of historical and scientific wonder and frustration, a
spiritual kingdom which nothing now can destroy. Don't
misjudge it. The spiritual kingdom opened up by Jesus is not
one which is so heavenly minded that it is of no earthly use. It
is the kingdom of God's love and righteousness which
reverses all human values and puts in place once and for all,
and here and now, the beginnings of all those ways which are
not our ways, the ways which belong to our peace, the ways
which bring to completion God's creative work (Isa. 55:8–13).

> Creator God,
> you turned chaos
> into your world
> of justice and trust,
> of hope and beauty,
> of truth and peace.
> We need you now,
> and your forgiveness,
> to rebuild what has been broken and destroyed.
> We need your heart of care and love
> to restore the lives of all your people,
> and bring your creation
> to the fulfilment and joy
> of your purposes and longing.

Evening meditation

Trust

> A darkness fell over the whole land, which lasted until
> three in the afternoon; the sun's light failed. And the
> curtain of the temple was torn in two. Then Jesus gave a
> loud cry and said, 'Father, into thy hands I commit my
> spirit'; and with these words he died. The centurion saw it

all, and gave praise to God. 'Beyond all doubt', he said,
'this man was innocent.'

Luke 23:44–47

Terry Waite and many other hostages have all had to face the
kind of deprivation which aims to reduce them to nothing.
Captivity and prison are intended to remove from the ego the
opportunities for action so that the personality steadily
collapses until it is unable to perform any action. Yet Jesus,
even in his final moments, did not lose all will-power or his
centre of self-awareness. He was still capable of action –
effective action – which would be as powerful as any that had
gone before.

It was widely believed in the early Church that Jesus had
said, 'It is more blessed to give than to receive.' Whether he
did or not, now at the end of his life, that is exactly what he
does. Significantly, giving is the final action of the Saviour of
the world. He gives himself into his Father's hands. At the
beginning of the end he had handed himself over to his
enemies, now he hands himself over to God. The same possibility will be ours – giving could be the very last thing we do.

We are sometimes surprised when we realize how little of
his teaching, if any, Jesus made up himself. This is not to say
he lacked originality and didn't break open wide new ground,
but his message and its interpretation was received through
his closeness to God, and all of it in one way or another is a
fulfilment of what he had learned from the Scriptures and the
history and experience of his people. Throughout the hours
on the cross Jesus repeated words he knew by heart: words
from Scripture which showed it was 'necessary that the
Christ should suffer these things and enter into his glory'
(Luke 24:26). Especially Jesus quoted from the religious songs
he knew from the books of Psalms.

In thee O Lord, have I put my trust:
>   let me never be put to confusion,
>   deliver me in thy righteousness.
Bow down thine ear to me: make haste to deliver me.
And be thou my strong rock, and house of defence:
>   that thou mayest save me.
For thou art my strong rock, and my castle:
>   be thou also my guide, and lead me for thy name's sake.
Draw me out of the net, that they have laid privily for me:
>   for thou art my strength.
Into thy hand I commit my spirit:
>   for thou hast redeemed me, O Lord, thou God of
>   truth.

Psalm 31:1–5

Jesus is no longer speaking into a terrible void and emptiness but once again consciously addressing his Father. His confidence and trust have already been renewed – broken and remade, matured and redefined, de-constructed and reconstructed. He is discovering that God is the one who both breaks down and builds up, who has torn that he may heal (Hos. 6:1). In that faith Jesus says, 'Father, into thy hands I commit my spirit.'

The same option can never be taken away from any human being. No outward circumstances can ever remove the possibility of such inward grace. The source of our being, the Spirit which God breathes into us at first, is indestructible and sustains us even as we go through death. There will never be a time or a place when we cannot give ourselves into God's hands. The divine–human relationship remains for ever mutual.

Through this confident act of self-giving and trust a legitimate contentment comes to Jesus, in which he wants all to share. 'None of us has power of ourselves to help ourselves' – not even Jesus – but God is with him, still enabling him to hold on to his true self and give it back to his Creator, articulating one of the inner certainties on which he had based all his prayers, his life in the Spirit, and his ministry – the knowledge that 'the Father had given all things into his hands, and that he had come from God and was going to God' (John 13:3). Jesus' words to others now apply to himself and he puts them into action. 'Anyone who loses his life for my sake and the gospel will receive it back again' (Mark 8:35).

Describing the divine work of creation, Scripture said, 'God rested on the seventh day' (Gen. 2:1–3), and, as we know, the Sabbath became a day of rest – the final day of the week. Yet every seventh day itself comes to an end and the cycle is endlessly repeated until a new purpose for it is brought to the world by Jesus. Now the rest he has in the Father's hands leads on to an eighth day, a day which lies beyond every other calculation and has no end. Into the eighth day, the day of resurrection, Jesus moves. Seeing Jesus taken down from the cross and laid in the tomb, his friends will be devastated but he will be given new life by God – life in all its fullness – which he gladly shares with all who dare to follow him.

Lord Jesus,
you completed your life and work
by giving yourself into your Father's hands:
be with us in all we do
in your name,
and help us
to give ourselves up
for the good news of the kingdom
and the praise of the Father's holy name.

Saturday in Holy Week

Sorrow turned to joy

Beginning to pray

Inside darkness, mists and uncertainty,
glimpses of shapes and hopes appear:
painfully and by making mistakes
we distinguish between
the real and the unreal,
the true and the false,
the firm stones of trust and the quicksand of delusion,
the strength of God with us
and the weakness of evil in defeat and withering away.

Bible reading

Let your bearing towards one another arise out of your life
in Christ Jesus. For the divine nature was his from the first;
yet he did not think to snatch at equality with God, but
made himself nothing, assuming the nature of a slave.
Bearing the human likeness, revealed in human shape, he
humbled himself, and in obedience accepted even death –
death on a cross. Therefore God raised him to the heights
and bestowed on him the name above all names, that at the
name of Jesus every knee should bow – in heaven, on earth,

and in the depths – and every tongue confess, 'Jesus Christ is Lord', to the glory of God the Father.

Philippians 2:5–11

Meditation

Josef Haydn wrote glorious music – operas, symphonies, quartets, *Creation* and other oratorios. He always said he owed his talent to his Creator, and in honour of God he is supposed to have put on his best coat whenever he was composing church music. His musical training began as a chorister, first in his local cathedral and then at the famous St Stephen's Cathedral in Vienna. He was known for his joyful and merry heart. As far as we know he enjoyed a long and fulfilled life, although when he married, it was, as we say, in haste. Sadly, it appears that he had time to repent at leisure.

Haydn was commissioned in 1785 to write a set of pieces for string quartet to be played in Cadiz Cathedral during the Good Friday Three Hours devotion based on the words of Jesus from the cross. When Haydn adapted the score for chorus, in his preface of 1801 he wrote, 'The task of writing seven adagios, each of which was to last about ten minutes, to preserve a connection between them without wearying the hearers, was none of the lightest.' His music proves that constraints can be very creative, especially in the hands of a great artist.

Sister Wendy Beckett recently gave another touching and little-known example in her TV programme *The Story of Painting*. The Dutch painter Vermeer, whose wonderful pictures are completely filled with calm and stillness, actually lived with considerable constraint, in a rather small house with his wife, eleven children and his mother-in-law!

A special kind of flowering often comes through

constraint. A gardener needs to prune his roses hard if they are to blossom at their best. We know sin stands in need of judgement, but we usually forget, or never realize, that goodness too must be judged if it is to yield its full harvest. 'Low lies the best till lifted up to heaven.'

At the beginning of Holy Week we said the constant human falling away from God has provided a definition of tragedy, and the return to God, our coming back to him, which he makes possible through the death of Jesus, belongs to the Divine Comedy. Within all the suffering, pain and death there is music to be heard by those with a keen ear, trained to listen and notice. Solemn music, but because of the victory achieved and celebrated by the cross, music also containing singing merrily on high, just as at Jesus' birth.

In the calendar Good Friday is sometimes not very far removed from April Fool's day, and occasionally both fall on the same day. St Paul called the great reversals in God's kingdom brought about by Jesus' ministry and death the foolishness of God (1 Cor. 1: 18–31). In God's kingdom the lost, the least and the last become the found, the greatest, and are placed first. The cross released God's sovereign activity in this world, which turns lives upside down and inside out, making fools of those who put trust in anything else.

If in prayers and thoughts through Holy Week we have moved from tragedy to comedy, then the terrible events of Jesus' passion redefine our concept of God and become a source of joy, blessing and renewal. Radically we adjust our ideas because of what Jesus suffers and how he dies. In the huddle of bones collapsed on the cross we see nothing of what we thought God would be like. Nevertheless *here is God*. Jesus is 'the higher gift than grace', God himself, a divinity refined in human flesh and blood in spite of all its fragility and impermanence. Here in this man and his death is

God's presence and his very Self,
And Essence all-divine.

One Palm Sunday morning the BBC's 'Week's Good Cause' was an appeal from a mother whose son had died tragically. She said, as all must know, 'No mother ever gets over the death of one of her own children.' Her simple words ring like a tolling bell. No mother ever gets over the death of her child – no – but then, nor, of course, does any father. On the cross God's own, dearly beloved Son was taken from him through wickedness, injustice and evil of every kind. We shall never know exactly what we have done to God in that action; which is one reason why there cannot be a final and complete understanding of either divine or human nature now, unless the life and death of Jesus is central to the search. In his story there is the highest act of self-giving we shall ever know, in a context where such an action was totally undeserved and unexpected. Human betrayal and rejection, folly and hate are matched by the opposite – divine love, continuous and unending, abundant giving, acceptance and welcome.

Do we not have to reckon here with a creator whose transcendence remains somehow inviolate, when he puts himself at the mercy of his creation? In Christ God is revealed as submitting himself to the very substance of human life, in its inexorable finitude, in its precarious ambiguity, in its movement to despair.

God is not the all-powerful, disinterested, unconnected life-force from beyond. He is the 'beyond in our midst' who suffers with us and is therefore to be trusted and adored.[9]

Song

> What wondrous love is this, O my soul, O my soul;
> What wondrous love is this
> That caused the Lord of bliss
> To bear the dreadful curse for my soul?
>
> To God and to the Lamb, I will sing, I will sing;
> To God and to the Lamb
> Who is the great I AM,
> While millions join the theme, I will sing.
>
> And when from death I'm free, I'll sing on, I'll sing on;
> And when from death I'm free
> I'll sing and joyful be,
> And through eternity I'll sing on.
>
> Early American folk song

Poem

> *Interruption to a Journey*
>
> The hare we had run over
> Bounced about the road
> On the springing curve
> Of its spine.
>
> Cornfields breathed in the darkness,
> We were going through the darkness and
> The breathing cornfields from one
> Important place to another.
>
> We broke the hare's neck
> And made that place, for a moment,
> The most important place there was,
> Where a bowstring was cut

And a bow broken forever
That had shot itself through so many
Darknesses and cornfields.

It was left in that landscape.
It left us in another.

Norman MacCaig

Prayers

Thanks be to thee, O Lord Jesus Christ,
for all the benefits which thou hast given us,
for all the pains and insults which thou hast borne for us.
O most merciful Redeemer,
Friend and Brother,
may we know thee more clearly,
love thee more dearly,
and follow thee more nearly,
day by day.

St Richard of Chichester

Praise to the Holiest in the height,
        And in the depth be praise,
In all his words most wonderful,
        Most sure in all his ways.

John Henry Newman

Part Two
Easter and After

Even as a small child, she had not believed, as others did, that heaven was in the stars, up and up above her, for there was something that frightened her in the night sky, a coldness, with only air rushing through the dark spaces between. No, she had always sensed that heaven was no further away than the tips of her own fingers, and if she were given eyes to see, it would be there, all about her and astonishingly familiar. She felt it now. If she reached out ...

Susan Hill, *In the Springtime of the Year*

Easter Week

Rejoice in the day the Lord has made

Beginning to pray

The Easter light shines,
proclaiming God's defeat of all that is evil
by the power of his self-giving love.
The same divine sovereignty gives Jesus life,
life renewed, life brought to fulfilment, life filled with
    glory.
God's dearly beloved Son is Christ and Saviour
for all creation and for ever.
Alleluia, alleluia.

Psalm

The Lord is my strength, and my song:
and has become my salvation.
The sounds of joy and deliverance:
are in the tents of the righteous.
The right hand of the Lord does mighty things:
the right hand of the Lord raises up.
I shall not die, but live:
and proclaim the works of the Lord.
The Lord has disciplined me hard:

but he has not given me over to death.
Open me the gates of righteousness:
and I will enter and give thanks to the Lord.

Psalm 118:14–19

Bible reading

When the Sabbath was over, Mary of Magdala, Mary the
mother of James, and Salome bought aromatic oils
intending to go and anoint the body of Jesus; and very
early on the Sunday morning, just after sunrise, they came
to the tomb. They were wondering among themselves who
would roll away the stone for them from the entrance to the
tomb, when they looked up and saw that the stone, huge as
it was, had been rolled back already. They went into the
tomb, where they saw a youth sitting on the right-hand
side, wearing a white robe; and they were dumbfounded.
But he said to them, 'Fear nothing; you are looking for
Jesus of Nazareth, who was crucified. He has been raised
again; he is not here; look, there is the place where they laid
him. But go and give this message to his disciples and Peter:
"He is going on before you into Galilee; there you will see
him, as he told you." ' Then they went out and ran away
from the tomb, beside themselves with terror. They said
nothing to anybody, for they were afraid.

Mark 16:1–8

(Additional readings: Luke 24:1–9; Colossians 3:1–4; 1
Peter 2:9; Isaiah 25:9.)

Song

The dark doubts of the winter months are past
And Easter, young and green is here at last.

The April morning grass is bless'd with dew
And palest sun shines out of palest blue.
The old sheep stroll, the young lambs leap and play.
O, blessed is the lamb newborn today.
The withered root entombed beneath the earth
Puts out new shoots and joins the great rebirth.
The Spring is here, the egg, the grain, the seed:
And from them the imprisoned life is freed;
From Winter's cold grave, Spring's new life appears
And echoes his resurrection through the years.

Katherine Middleton

Prayer

In your heart, in the place where no two people are ever alike, Christ is waiting for you. And what you never dared hope for springs to life.

Brother Roger of Taizé

Take time to be still and attentive. Receive the message of hope and know the presence of the risen Christ with you. Look for the gift of serenity and a quiet mind, and allow the truth of Easter to overcome your anxieties and fears, your sin and frailty. Take hold of this 'new life' with joy and thankfulness.

Pray by name for those who are in need of any kind. Ask that they too may share joy in the forgiveness and the healing power of the resurrection.

Jesus greets his friends with his gift of peace: 'Peace be with you; my peace I give you.' Pray for the world and pray by name for places where there is conflict and violence.

Prayer

> Loving God, Father and Maker of all;
> you gave your Son new life
> and brought him out of darkness and death
> to live for ever:
> bring us with him
> out from the dark places surrounding us,
> and raise us
> to be with Jesus our Lord,
> in the power of your Life,
> today and always.

Meditations

Song for a new world

When a composer writes a piece of music his work is not over when he has thought of a good tune. He also needs a good rhythm to go with it, to carry the melody. Some pieces sound all tune, like Handel's great Easter aria 'I know that my redeemer liveth', while others seem to be all rhythm, like Ravel's famous 'Bolero', which brought Torville and Dean to the heights of their career on ice. Listen carefully, though, and you will hear both melody and rhythm present in each piece, because more often than not they are inseparable.

On Easter Day the melody is 'Jesus lives!' Everything round sings the same tune: the spring sunshine, the beauty of the daffodils and cherry blossom, the natural joy and vitality of a bank-holiday weekend (sometimes in spite of the rain). The song of the world and the chanting of Christians fit together:

> Jesus lives! thy terrors now
>   Can, O Death, no more appal us.

The exhilarating Easter melody though is sustained by a definite rhythm which has been set beating in Holy Week and during the weeks of Lent. It's the same rhythm which we first hear in Christian baptism; the rhythm of dying in order to live, of giving in order to receive, of losing in order to find. The regular discipline of self-giving and self-emptying underpins the whole Christian life, in large and small acts of personal sacrifice and obedience, and for all whose living sounds with it, the rhythm releases their share of Easter joy.

Everyone knows it isn't easy to believe in the resurrection, especially for those who have not yet made every Sunday a day of Jesus' resurrection and every act of worship a meeting with the risen Lord. Such folk have not discovered how new *every morning* is God's love. For them the grand, majestic, triumph of Easter Day is not yet built on strong foundations and reinforced in daily life.

Sometimes people blame the times we live in, though each generation in every age has found Easter incredible rather than credible and difficult to take in. It isn't the scientific mind, or secular man, or the historian, or the post-modernist as such who finds it difficult to believe in resurrection. When the three Marys went to the tomb on the first Easter morning they were terrified by what they had seen, and they had then to find their individual way to belief. Saint Paul recognized that faith in the power of God to bring life out of death was foolishness to the Greeks and a stumbling block to Jews (I Cor. I:23), just as it raises opposition in Senior Common Rooms and in TV discussions and documentaries today.

Believing in resurrection is always beyond the regularly used intellectual capacity of human beings, but to say so is not to take the easy way out of a difficulty. It doesn't imply that wrestling with faith is unnecessary or irrelevant. Far from it. All who witness the way God brings light out of darkness need to use imagination, experience, prayer, listening to others, and careful and detailed study, including Bible study, to understand what is happening. It can sometimes take only a moment to know the truth and be grasped by it, but it always takes a lifetime to work out the implications and found it firmly on understanding. Everyone who sings 'Christ is risen' fights hard, each in his or her own individual way, to learn how they can take up the theme lustily with honesty and conviction.

> Risen Lord and Master,
> give us faith
> to open our minds and release our imagination,
> to recognize your presence,
> to know you are here
> and to rejoice in God's power
> of life over death.
> Alleluia!

Broken and healed

Even if we admit that those who don't sufficiently practise living in the presence of the Living Lord find it hard to believe in Easter, there is another difficulty to be faced which goes much deeper.

Someone once said, 'The question, "Do you believe in the resurrection?" is really another question in disguise – "Have you experienced what it is like to be broken and healed? Do you know what it's like to die the death of shame, or disappointment, or hurt pride, and then somehow come back to life?" ' Many do have this experience. Some have the experience but don't go on and build faith on it.

Once find joy returning after sorrow, in a personal, private matter, and the whole structure of the gospel not only stands on firmer convictions but is also given a coherence which makes much good sense.[10]

Such inner experience and the personal strength, perceptions and understanding which it brings with it is all part of the proof and the continuing elucidation of Easter. Or if you think proof is the wrong word, then say such experience provides the evidence which must be weighed to discover and establish the probabilities for Easter faith, and the sure and certain hope it proclaims.

When the women went to the garden to tend Jesus' corpse, they wondered how they would move the stone away from the entrance to the grave. They need not have worried. When they arrived, the stone had *already* been rolled away. The word 'already' is one of the greatest words in the Christian good news. God had *already* acted and life had *already* moved on to a new place and into the new world which had arrived through divine grace and power. The women and all Jesus' friends had to catch up with God, who had yet again gone on ahead of them.

He is such a fast
God, always before us and
leaving as we arrive.[11]

We often have to run simply to stand still in this world made and sustained by a divine love which moves so fast that to be with God is beyond our strength. Thankfully, not only does God choose to come to be with us, but also Jesus takes us with him to be with God, if we will allow him to move us forward at his pace rather than our own.

Rise heart; thy Lord is risen. Sing his praise
    Without delayes,
Who takes thee by the hand, that thou likewise
    With him mayst rise:
That, as his death calcined thee to dust,
His life may make thee gold, and much more, just.

Awake, my lute, and struggle for thy part
    With all thy art.
The crosse taught all wood to resound his name,
    Who bore the same.
His stretched sinews taught all strings, what key
Is best to celebrate this most high day.

Consort both heart and lute, and twist a song
    Pleasant and long:
Or, since all musick is but three parts vied
    And multiplied,
O let thy blessed Spirit bear a part,
And make up our defects with his sweet art.

              George Herbert (1593–1633)

Finally notice that belief in resurrection makes great demands on the human intellect, emotions and will precisely because faith is always a gift. Again, in this matter, 'we have no power of ourselves to help ourselves.' To sing 'Jesus Christ is risen today' and to be able to share in the symbolism and reality of being buried in the waters of baptism and then live the new life of the Spirit is God's free gift to us, rather than a concept or an experience which we construct for ourselves or from within ourselves. Such a statement raises profound and unavoidable philosophical questions, but I continue to believe that there is truth which we do not spin out of our own gut, however resourceful we may become, and it is this kind of truth we are offered through faith in the Risen Christ. Truth which holds us by its own inherent, reasonable and imaginative power.

Risen Lord,
touch our lives
with healing, forgiveness and newness
that we may know again the fullness
and glory of the Father's promise
that all things are blessed and redeemed
by his goodness.
Alleluia!

Second Week of Easter

Spring is here to stay

Beginning to pray

After weeping and sorrow,
in the morning dawn
another day breaks out
offering new opportunities
    with many chances to begin again.
In the freshness God seeks us,
inviting us to find him in Jesus – the risen Lord;
for Mary and for us
the teacher who shows
the everlasting love and forgiveness
of his Father:
and ours.

Psalm

When the Lord turned again the fortunes of Zion:
    then were we like those restored to life.
Then was our mouth filled with laughter:
    and our tongue with singing.
Then said they among the heathen:
    'The Lord has done great things for them.'

Truly the Lord has done great things for us:
> and therefore we rejoiced.

Turn again our fortunes, O Lord:
> as the streams return to the dry south.

Those who sow in tears:
> shall reap with songs of joy.

They that go out weeping, bearing the seed:
> shall come again in gladness,
>> bringing their sheaves with them.

Psalm 126

Bible reading

Mary stood weeping outside the tomb, and as she wept she stooped to look into the tomb; and she saw two angels in white, sitting where the body of Jesus had lain, one at the head and one at the feet. They said to her, 'Woman, why are you weeping?' She said to them, 'Because they have taken away my Lord, and I do not know where they have laid him.' Saying this, she turned round and saw Jesus standing, but she did not know that it was Jesus. Jesus said to her, 'Woman, why are you weeping? Whom do you seek?' Supposing him to be the gardener, she said to him, 'Sir, if you have carried him away, tell me where you have laid him, and I will take him away.' Jesus said to her, 'Mary.' She turned and said to him in Hebrew, '*Rab-bo'ni!*' (which means 'Teacher'). Jesus said to her, 'Do not hold me, for I have not yet ascended to the Father; but go to my brethren and say to them, "I am ascending to my Father and your Father, to my God and your God." ' Mary Mag'dalene went and said to the disciples, 'I have seen the Lord'; and she told them that he had said these things to her.

John 20:11–18

(Additional readings: Colossians 3:1–4; Isaiah 55:3–5.)

Song

When the hour comes,
you shall change my desert into a waterfall,
you shall anoint my head with fresh oil
and your strength shall overcome my weakness.
You shall guide my feet into your footsteps
and I will walk the narrow path
that leads to your house.

You shall tell me when
and where
I will walk your path
totally bathed in joy.
In the meantime,
I ask you Lord, you who awaken
in the most intimate place in my soul
the Feast of Life!
That of the Empty Tomb!
That of the Victorious Cross!

Let your voice mistaken as the Gardener's
awaken my hearing every morning
with news that's always fresh:
'Go and tell the others
that I have overcome death,
and that there is a place for everyone

there where the New Nation is built.'

Julia Esquival

Prayer

Christ comes through our frailties, our inner nights, giving them something of his presence. He transforms the deepest parts of us. He transfigures them.

Brother Roger of Taizé

Look for the goodness of God, in the beauty of creation, in the wonder and uniqueness of each part of creation, in people who surround others with love and friendship, in family and among partners and companions.

Try to contemplate ways in which such goodness overcomes the evil which is also in human life.

Think more deeply about the presence of God; which means thinking about the signs we have which indicate his presence, signs in the world and in other people, in history and experience.

Consider how easily these signs are mistaken and go unrecognized:

- Mary mistook Jesus for a gardener.

- Their conversation together started with a series of misunderstandings.

- It was Jesus who broke through the circles of missed meaning and restored recognition between them and Mary's relationship with him.

- Consider how muddled and impatient you become sometimes when you try to find God and be with him.

Finally give to God your emptiness and darkness: and ask him to shine within it. Then be willing to wait if necessary before things come clear again.

Prayer

> Lord Jesus,
> you spoke to Mary in the garden
> and gave her back her faith and hope in God.
> Help us to be prepared to wait long enough
> to seek you, to find you, and to recognize you;
> then draw us nearer to God
> and keep us with you every day
> as we come to know more fully
> the glory of the Father.

Meditations

Vision and truth

On 8 May 1373, Julian of Norwich received her vision, or 'shewings', of the divine love. Mother Julian's experience was intense and immeasurably creative both for her and for all who have read her accounts of the shewings. It may be a surprise though to know that the occasion was also short, lasting not much more than about five hours.[12] During the rest of her life, as far as we know, no further vision was given to her. We might have thought that once a state of ecstasy was achieved it would remain at least a semi-permanent condition; but no, that rarely, if ever, happens. Instead, Mother Julian's remaining years were fully occupied 'unpacking' the mystical experience of God's loving which had refreshed her and given her a vigorous and demanding new start on that memorable day. Much came from such a brief encounter. Going deeper into the divine love day by day and entering its mystery provided all the nourishment and strength she needed for faith. For forty years or more, she held her never-to-be-forgotten moment of revelation and ecstasy side by side with the mundane, necessary and often tedious duties of daily life. Significantly, they did not cancel each other out or war with each other. Both were equally valuable in the life of the Spirit, validating and illuminating each other.

Like the vision of Julian of Norwich, the annual Christian celebration of the cross and resurrection was originally equally intense and brief. It was not spread over the weeks of Lent and Holy Week, but took place in the few hours of darkness and dawn on Easter Eve.[13] What happened is contained in the Easter liturgy, one of the richest parts of the Christian heritage we have. The central moment included the baptism of new believers. In this intense and powerful symbol, they shared the fundamental experience of Easter and received the new life of the risen Jesus, by going with him into his death (Rom. 6:3–11). Afterwards, the remaining years of discipleship, witness and service became a working out of the fresh start made in the 'moment' of paschal baptism; years which were sustained and interpreted by the regular breaking of bread and drinking the cup. Baptism and Eucharist are both rooted in Easter life, which they interpret and sustain.

At the time of her vision, Mother Julian had been seriously ill for about a week. She and others thought her death was near. Certainly, she was vulnerable to suggestion. The sceptic might say this accounts for the vision and dismiss it as entirely subjective: hallucinations brought on by sickness and the fear of dying. It could be; but if so, such an explanation is completely inadequate for the remarkable life Mother Julian went on to live in Norwich – a life which has produced so many good things and spiritual depth in the lives of those who read her writings, especially in our own time. A sceptical account simply cannot explain the integrity of her witness to

Christ or the results which flow from what happened to her. A religious experience with such lasting value and energy in its outcome needs more than delirium and wish-fulfilment as its cause.

At least some of the same qualities belong to all experiences of the risen Jesus – they are likely to be intense, quite short and immediate; they will be easily misunderstood; the sceptical observer will quickly find ways of explaining them away; an 'outsider' will need to look hard to find ways of communicating with the recipient of the experience; and yet, when the experiences are authentic they will produce such startling and tangible results that only an acceptance of the reality of resurrection will adequately account for them. Above all, they will remain central to the life of those now living in the known presence of the risen Lord and create unending nourishment and strength for themselves and for others.

Risen Lord,
    be with me in the power of your new life.
Open me that I may grow in the Spirit
    in love and understanding
    in knowledge and self-giving.
Let me receive your strength
    that I may accept the trials
    which I must endure with you.
Help me to treasure the revelations you bring
    of the presence and power
    of God.
Give me the refreshment
    of a new beginning
    in his joy and glory.

Life ablaze with God

In the garden on Easter morning, Mary Magdalene was completely broken and empty. Her psyche was as vulnerable and open to suggestion as Mother Julian's, sick and facing death. Mary went in a state of shock and overwhelming grief, looking for all that remained of her much-loved Master, which she believed would be a corpse. After receiving the literally incredible news of resurrection, she lingered and stayed behind among the trees, caught between despair and hope, between fear and joy. Could such a claim ever be true?

Then Jesus was with her. Of course she didn't recognize him because her mind and imagination were still fixed by her expectation of finding a dead body. She saw something else: a person, living and present. Not for a moment did she think she was seeing a ghost or that her senses were misleading her. The world was still there and real enough. Whatever was happening, she knew she was not out of her mind (though others might think she was and would probably say she was). Jesus was dead, so who else could it be but a gardener, the only person who might be about at the time, working in the garden? The quality of stark, utter realism which possessed Mary throughout that day is central to what happened to her in the Easter garden and how it took place.[14]

Though Mary didn't recognize him, Jesus recognized Mary and addressed her by name. That was the turning point. His action became the point of connection between the power of God to bring good out of evil and the receiving of new, restored life by Mary. Notice how Jesus' recognition of her, rather than her recognition of him, healed Mary, brought her back from grief and gave her new hope.

Some religious experience is indeed hallucinatory and

therefore dangerous and misleading. We should be suspicious and reject it. But much more religious experience comes from God and is life-giving and glorious. Mary Magdalene in the garden, Mother Julian in her cell – both were clearly gripped by genuine, life-giving, religious experience. They couldn't have lived the rest of their lives as they did if what happened to them had been an empty deception. Nothing less than the divine life and the divine love in all its creative power were known to them when the crucified and risen Lord Jesus was present with them.

Christian faith develops and strengthens when we accept that it is a gift, rather than a construction of our own making. We can find shapes and patterns within faith which fit and make good sense, but they *follow* rather than originate experience. Searching for the life of the Spirit in our fumbling, ill-informed ways, we are often completely shut down and empty in heart, mind and spirit. Then the risen Jesus is with us, seeking us out with his knowledge of us rather than our knowledge of him and calling us to move forward out of the dark shadows of uncertainty into the kingdom of his Father.

Individual religious experience may well be a brief encounter. What matters is not its duration but its intensity and its origin, whether or not it comes from God. Jesus' words and conversation in the garden placed Mary in the sphere of God's kingdom where suffering, resurrection and glory make sense. Then, like Mother Julian, she used the rest of her life to work out the implications of her brief and intense vision. To each disciple the risen Jesus speaks as he places them in the sphere of resurrection life. A moment of revelation sets the whole world and every day ablaze with God.

Risen Lord and Master,
    you know me better than I know myself;
    speak and help me to listen;
    call me into your life,
    that with you I may possess your Father's kingdom.
Give me insight to recognize you
    in the moment of your speaking,
    and to value the time of your calling;
that through all my days
    I may rejoice with you
    in the power of God,
    and receive a share in the glory
    of his victory and love.

Third Week of Easter

Strangers

Beginning to pray

Travelling day by day through the world,
taking large and small journeys,
sometimes after careful plans are laid,
sometimes unexpectedly with no preparations,
meeting others along every path,
encounters with friends, acquaintances and strangers:
God is in those who walk with us
    and in those we meet.
We need open eyes
    to recognize God in them;
we need open hands to help
    and serve God in them;
we need to recognize Jesus is with us
    to enjoy the friendship and love of God,
    and to know his presence in our midst.

Psalm

Blessed are those whose help is the God of Jacob:
    whose hope is in the Lord their God,
The God who made heaven and earth:

the sea, and all that is in them,
Who keeps faith for ever:
>who deals justice to those that are oppressed.
The Lord gives food to the hungry:
>and sets the captives free.
The Lord gives sight to the blind:
>the Lord lifts up those that are bowed down.
The Lord loves the righteous:
>the Lord cares for the stranger in the land.
He upholds the widow and fatherless:
>as for the way of the wicked, he turns it upside down.
The Lord shall be king for ever:
>your God, O Zion, shall reign through all
>>generations.
>Praise the Lord.

Psalm 146:5–10

Bible reading

That very day two of them were going to a village named Emmaus, about seven miles from Jerusalem, and talking with each other about all these things that had happened. While they were talking and discussing together, Jesus himself drew near and went with them. But their eyes were kept from recognizing him. And he said to them, 'What is this conversation which you are holding with each other as you walk?' And they stood still, looking sad. Then one of them, named Cleopas, answered him, 'Are you the only visitor to Jerusalem who does not know the things that have happened there in these days?' And he said to them, 'What things?' And they said to him, 'Concerning Jesus of Nazareth, who was a prophet mighty in deed and word before God and all the people, and how our chief priests and rulers delivered him up to be condemned to death, and crucified him. But we had hoped that he was the one to redeem Israel. Yes, and besides all this, it is now the third day since this happened. Moreover, some women of our company amazed us. They were at the tomb early in the morning and did not find his body; and they came back saying that they had even seen a vision of angels, who said that he was alive. Some of those who were with us went to the tomb, and found it just as the women had said; but him they did not see.' And he said to them, 'O foolish men, and slow of heart to believe all that the prophets have spoken! Was it not necessary that the Christ should suffer these things and enter into his glory?' And beginning with Moses and all the prophets, he interpreted to them in all the scriptures the things concerning himself.

Luke 24:13–27

(Additional readings: Ephesians 2:12–22; Isaiah 25:9.)

Song

It's darker now, but there is light within us;
We faced the sundown, yet our dawn has come.
Our heavy feet dragged on the westward journey
Which now are swift, for every place is home.

We came in sorrow, but in joy returning
We tread the same road, though with different eyes;
Hasten to share with others this new wonder,
Recall his promises that he would rise.

We did not know Him as He walked beside us,
Yet our hearts kindled at the words he said –
Slow to believe the truths we so much longed for,
But quick to know those loved hands broke the bread.

It was the Lord, whom we had thought a stranger.
How dim our eyes! But now, with faith restored,
At any turn of roadway we may meet him,
In any stranger we may see the Lord.

Lucy M. Green

Prayer

The more we share what we have, in a spirit of great simplicity, the more life becomes welcoming for those who have been entrusted to us.

Brother Roger of Taizé

Stand for a few moments with open hands as though to receive a gift. Ask God to open your heart and mind in the same way to receive what he is giving you.

Then sit or kneel quietly and be silent before asking God to help you to know him in others: your family and friends, your companions and those with whom you work. Try to attend to any particular need they have and decide to do what you can to help.

Think then of those who remain strange to you; those you do not yet know; those you perceive as alien – offensive, even; those you cannot understand and for whom you have no sympathy.

Use the words 'compassion' and 'companion' to explore further how God brings together friend and stranger into a company. Ask for sympathy and fellowship to grow within you. Allow the risen Jesus to draw these things out of you.

Finally thank God for his glad acceptance of you – just as you are – and the delight which he takes in your loving him and all he has created.

Prayer

> Lord Jesus
> journey with us;
> heal our blindness,
> restore our ability to listen and hear,
> give us the insight to recognize you
> in those we meet,
> so that in them we may give you welcome.
> Break bread with us
> and create your fellowship among us.
> Then bring us to the Father's kingdom
> of joy and hope and peace.

Meditations

The kingdom of heaven open to all believers

Often when we see them out of place and in an unexpected context, we fail to recognize our friends. In new circumstances even our best friends can appear strangers to us for a moment. This may be why the New Testament accounts of the appearances of the risen Jesus to his friends record the many times they did not immediately recognize him – Mary Magdalene in the garden (John 20:14); the two travellers on the way to Emmaus (Luke 24:16); the disciples when they saw a figure on the shore by the lake (John 21:4 & 12). Later, when he saw the risen Jesus, St Paul asked, 'Who are you, Lord?' (Acts 9:5).

Jesus would not have deliberately confused his friends. What seems to have happened is that they could not easily connect *the risen Lord* with Jesus as they had known him and with whom they had shared so much. Jesus transfigured and raised in the Father's kingdom was not only more than they had ever dreamed or imagined he could be, but now required from them new vision and radical new depth of understanding of everything about him. He was barely recognizable after Easter because the whole context of his presence with the disciples had changed. Appearing among them in the fullness of the resurrection, Jesus was known yet unknown, familiar yet strange.

In Paris, around the quire of Notre-Dame, there is a stone screen with two sets of remarkable fourteenth-century carvings. The north side shows the humanity of Jesus. The south side shows his resurrection life. In the beautiful sculptures of the Easter appearances we see the disciples discovering how the loving memories they had of Jesus fitted with the glory he now possessed in the kingdom, breaking in at last on earth as it is in heaven.

In the scenes the sculptor has carved, each person comes to recognize the risen Lord in their own time and in their own way, and each time Jesus helps them to make the leap of faith. Jesus takes trouble to reveal to his friends the continuities between himself as he was and as he is now in his risen life. None of the appearances is gratuitous or an indulgence, each has a definite purpose. He speaks to each person according to their condition and need. To Mary he says, 'Do not cling to me' (John 20:17); to Thomas he says, 'Reach your finger here; see my hands. Reach your hand here and put it into my side' (John 20:27); to the disciples he says, 'Shoot the net to starboard, and you will make a catch' (John 21:6); to Peter he says, 'Feed my sheep' (John 21:15–17); to Paul he says, 'I appoint you my servant and witness' (Acts 26:12–18). Everything about Jesus after Easter is specific and direct. His words are spoken one to one, creating and demanding a response, making a personal invitation to believe and act.

Whenever the disciples began to recognize the risen Jesus

with them, they experienced divine power bringing the kingdom to birth through resurrection. As recognition came to them, they saw and believed and a revolution in thought and prayer and behaviour took place. The same movement takes place in us. We can easily make their mistake, what might be called a 'category mistake', and place Jesus in the familiar world of where he was in Palestine instead of placing him where he is now, in the sphere of the resurrection. Then it will be hard to believe and understand Easter. But if, like the disciples, our hearts and minds become better attuned to the coming of God's kingdom, then Jesus will no longer be strange to us. We shall recognize his presence and hear his voice speaking.

> Risen Lord Jesus
> open my eyes to see you
> open my mind to know you
> open my heart to your loving;
> speak to me as I am
> show me what you want me to be
> strengthen me to do whatever task you set me,
> and stay close to me
> always.

Signs and presence

The two men who walked so disconsolately from Jerusalem to Emmaus after the shattering events of Good Friday show in their story one way in which many people first encounter both the fact and the meaning of Easter Day.

What happened is well known. Somewhere along the journey a stranger joined them and walked with them; someone who could read their thoughts. Gradually he revealed to them the straight lines and patterns of truth which were being hidden and obscured by the tangles inside their minds and broken hearts. The New Testament says, 'he explained to them the passages which referred to [the messiah] in every part of the scriptures' (Luke 24:27). The stranger was a source of understanding and inspiration. He became precious to them. Then instead of parting from him at the division of the roads, they invited him to stay, thereby giving themselves the opportunity to be with him long enough to know the moment of miracle – when he broke bread they recognized the presence of Jesus and knew him to be the risen Lord.

Many come to a knowledge of resurrection in the same way. Unplanned and unexpected, another person is often the one who puts the chaos of our thoughts into perspective so that we can make sense of them. Afterwards, a pattern emerges quite clearly. By beginning to attend again more carefully to the meaning of tradition and by sharing in the sacrament of the Eucharist, we come to see and believe resurrection for ourselves.

Whenever they recognized him and saw the Lord, the disciples were glad – a joy we can well understand. But Easter invites a double act of recognition. We not only have to recognize the glory of God in Jesus and acknowledge him as Christ, the agent and bringer of the kingdom, but also we have to recognize and celebrate the same glory of God being brought to birth in other people as in ourselves.

Sometimes the second task is the more difficult one. Other people and even our own being can seem alien and remain 'strange' to us. An actual stranger we may meet will mirror this basic fact. Strangers are rarely easy to be with. We do not quickly confide in them or readily give them our trust. Yet they are those who can carry the Easter gospel and bring us revelation. Always they offer another starting point in our thinking and doing. They invite new perspectives, new decisions, new actions. Strangers in our midst are often those who open us to God and bring us into his presence because he is the One who cares for the outsider and the rejected.

The movement of peoples from place to place has continued throughout history – sometimes they have been refugees, sometimes migrants, sometimes adventurers looking for wealth or conquest. In recent years the speed with which people have moved around the world has greatly accelerated. Now, in virtually every country there are 'strangers' living in the midst – people from other countries and other cultures, with different language and religion. They are shopping, travelling, working and being educated alongside those who are native. We meet all kinds of strangers very regularly nowadays. In Christ our response will be hospitality and welcome rather than suspicion precisely because of the potential they carry and the messages they bring.

Jesus came as a stranger to the two disciples on the road to Emmaus while they were searching for meaning. They were asking the universal question formed by grief – Why? Whatever other things Jesus may have said to them to bring hope and strength in their sorrow, he must have demonstrated and explained the corporate meaning of resurrection. Jesus knew his Father had not given him new life just for his own sake. Jesus could not be raised alone. God's purpose in resurrection is that through his new life Jesus will bring others to the kingdom with him. 'Christ was raised to life – the first-fruits of the harvest' (1 Cor. 15:20).

Living Lord,
be with us in our daily journey:
teach us to value and treasure our joys;

comfort and relieve our sorrows,
open our hearts and minds
to know your presence with us
in both friend and stranger.
As you saw your Father
in all whom you met
and who came to you in their need,
help us to understand and hear
God's message of love and forgiveness
which others bring.

Fourth Week of Easter

The meal with the Lord

Beginning to pray

Call the children and family, the table is ready,
the food waiting to be served.
Call the guests and friends,
call the strangers and those in need.
For we must share what we are given:
the Lord God is found in harvest and famine,
and the risen Christ is in the man and woman and child
who is placed with us,
sits next as neighbour,
and comes to us for help.

Psalm

God has stood up in the council of heaven:
    in the midst of the gods he gives judgement.
'How long will you judge unjustly:
    and favour the cause of the wicked?
Judge for the poor and fatherless:
    vindicate the afflicted and oppressed.
Rescue the poor and needy:
    and save them from the hands of the wicked.

They do not know, they do not understand,
>   they walk about in darkness:
>   all the foundations of the earth are shaken.
Therefore I say, "Though you are gods:
>   and all of you children of the Most High,
nevertheless you shall die like a mortal:
>   and fall like one of the princes." '
Arise, O God, judge the earth:
>   and you shall take all nations as your possession.

Psalm 82

Bible reading

When they got out on land, they saw a charcoal fire there, with fish lying on it, and bread. Jesus said to them, 'Bring some of the fish that you have just caught.' So Simon Peter went aboard and hauled the net ashore, full of large fish, a hundred and fifty-three of them; and although there were so many, the net was not torn. Jesus said to them, 'Come and have breakfast.' Now none of the disciples dared to ask him, 'Who are you?' They knew it was the Lord. Jesus came and took the bread and gave it to them, and so with the fish. This was now the third time that Jesus was revealed to the disciples after he was raised from the dead.

John 21:9–14

(Additional readings: Acts 2:42–47; 1 Kings 17:13–16.)

Song

Come on,
Let us celebrate the supper of the Lord.
Let us make a huge loaf of bread
and let us bring abundant wine
like at the wedding at Cana.

Let the women not forget the salt.
Let the men bring along the yeast.
Let many guests come,
the lame, the blind, the crippled, the poor.

Come quickly.
Let us follow the recipe of the Lord.
All of us, let us knead the dough together
with our hands.
Let us see with joy
how the bread grows.

Because today
we celebrate
the meeting with the Lord.
Today we renew our commitment
to the Kingdom.
Nobody will stay hungry.

Elsa Tamez

Prayer

*Alleviating human suffering is engraved at the heart of the
Gospel. And when we allay other people's trials, we do it
for Christ; and still more – it is the Risen Christ that we
encounter.*

Brother Roger of Taizé

Hold together in your heart and will your offering of worship
and the desire to serve others. Ask God to help you see both
as aspects of the same relationship – being with him in
adoration and self-giving.

By whatever means, learn of the needs of others, particularly those who are close to you as neighbour day after day.

Open your heart to them and ask God to show you what to
do to help.

Then think of all the many people who give help, indivi-
duals and agencies and groups. Pray for their work and
resolve that your prayer and love for God will not run into the
sand but will be channelled into practical help.

Prayer

Lord Jesus, you gathered your friends together
at breakfast beside the lake
for a simple meal,
as you did at supper the night before you died,
to remember and celebrate
the power of God to rescue and save:
you showed them
the inward meaning and grace of your Father's power –
love given out to others to serve and heal.
Host us now;
help us to rejoice with all those you have given to us
as brothers and sisters;
and help us to be gracious companions
and serve one another
for your name's sake.

Meditations

Gathered and scattered

I found a saying unexpectedly quoted for encouragement in a
cookery book: 'A good meal makes a person feel more chari-
table toward the whole world than any sermon.' An exagger-
ation perhaps and untheological, but below the surface there
is a pointer to the true significance of every meal.

Meals are times of fellowship as well as appetite. People gather together around a table and relate to each other for better – and sometimes for worse, it has to be admitted. A meal can be at least an opportunity for those being fed to think about others who have little or nothing, and hopefully then to be moved by conscience to go on and share hospitality and sustenance with people in need. A simple community meal is at the heart of both Christianity and Judaism. Medieval Christians were said to taste God on their tongues, and in the Middle Ages, Jewish rabbis sometimes asked for their coffins to be made out of planks of their kitchen tables. After Easter, Jesus' risen presence was often revealed to the disciples during a meal. These meals with the Lord drew them closer to God and to each other, evoking in various ways both worship and morality.

Sharing bread and wine is a universal symbol of hospitality for all time. Even the simple gesture of offering a visitor a cup of coffee or tea and a biscuit – food and drink – is a basic human instinct. Whoever we welcome in such ways immediately receives in greater or less measure, from another person, acceptance, interest, openness, care and the possibility of concern – the good qualities received when we are in a relationship which enable men and women to be as God intended and as they would wish to be.

The post-Easter meals which Jesus enjoyed with his friends were times of rejoicing and celebration, in complete contrast to the solemn meal he shared with them on the last night of his earthly life, full of brooding and desperate apprehension. Some scholars have argued strongly that these meals, with their obvious joy given through the presence of the risen Lord, are the proper origin of the Christian Eucharist, rather than the Last Supper.[15] They say St Paul later used memories and the reported pattern of what happened during the final

Passover meal of Jesus with the twelve to add another layer of interpretation and meaning to what the first Christians already believed about the Eucharist, based on the many times they had spent in thanksgiving to God in the presence of the risen Lord.

The meal with the Lord has built into it an unending, powerful dynamic. Wherever we put the emphasis – on celebration or sacrifice, on resurrection or crucifixion, on Jesus' coming to us in the breaking of bread or on his going to the Father by way of giving his life-blood on the cross – the Christian Eucharist meal in all its diversity provides the central and directing focus for Christian faith and discipleship. Karl Barth said that at the Eucharist the people of God gather round the table of the Lord for worship, and from it they are scattered for mission and service.

> Risen Master,
> call us again and again to your table
> and to the feast of your Father's kingdom.
> Give us joy in our hearts
> and make us aware of those around us
> with whom we break bread;
> help us to draw in
> those still outside this circle of friends.
> In our thanksgiving
> make us eager to share
> all we so much enjoy
> and have gratefully received
> with any who arrive at our door,
> and all who seek and need our help.
> So that all creation may reach the resurrection
> which begins in you.

Celebration and commissioning

Once Jesus met the disciples and shared a meal with them
while they were working on the Sea of Tiberias. He called out
from the shore to encourage them in their fishing (John
21:1–12). Then, back on land, he invited them to come and
have breakfast, and there is at least a hint that he cooked it
himself, making a fire and using bread he had brought with
the fish they had caught.

The mutual fellowship of Master and friends is expressed
and made powerfully present whenever Jesus breaks bread
with us. Through bread and wine Jesus opens our eyes,
sometimes gradually, sometimes in a flash of disclosure, so
that we grow enough to receive a better understanding of
resurrection.

A meal obviously offers more than fellowship, however
enjoyable. A meal gives refreshment, providing sustenance
and energy for future work. The meals which the disciples
enjoyed with the Lord equipped them for their task of being
the Church in the world. On this occasion the meal with the
Lord was breakfast, a meal *before* rather than after work.
Afterwards Jesus gave Peter his new task, 'feed my sheep'
(John 21:15–17). Having made himself known to his friends,
as he had done in his earthly ministry, Jesus then sent them
out as his companions to do his work. Every Eucharist is a
celebration and also a commissioning.

The period of time after Easter – eucharistic time, we
could call it; a time of thanksgiving; time during which we
share meals with the Lord – is an interim period. It is the time
between the resurrection of Jesus and the final incoming of
God's kingdom in which all creation will share. Jesus was not
raised by God into the fullness of the kingdom in splendid
isolation. The risen Jesus is now bringing his friends and

eventually all creation with him to God. Somehow, in God's own time and in his own way, all will be brought by the Son to the Father.

At the Edinburgh Festival one year, Sir Alec Guinness played in T. S. Eliot's play *The Cocktail Party*. He remembers coming out of the theatre after an evening performance and meeting a woman who thanked him for it. 'Did you understand the play?' he asked gently. 'No,' she replied, 'but I *enjoyed* it very much!' Lack of understanding, either complete or partial, is not necessarily a barrier to participation and enjoyment.

Part of the life-giving mystery of Christianity is that full understanding is not a prerequisite for receiving the blessing and fruitfulness of the experience. We may never understand entirely what happens in the meals we share with the risen Lord, but by participation we are given strong and lasting nourishment. When Queen Elizabeth I was asked what happens in the sacramental meal of Christians, she gave a famous reply which is still profound and more than adequate:

> ' 'Twas God the word that spake it,
> He took the bread and brake it;
> And what the word did make it;
> That I believe, and take it.'

Lord Jesus,
give us your strength and vision
when we share bread and wine
with you and one another.
Help us to know you are present
wherever the Father's kingdom is among us:
in blessings received and in needs still being filled,
in the work of compassion and care,
in the thirst and struggle for justice and peace.

Take whatever we can bring
and put it with all you are and give.
Set us to be your companions
in the work you ask of us,
and give us your Spirit,
that we may go with your joy
in our hearts,
and your risen power
in our lives.

Fifth Week of Easter

Harvest of peace

Beginning to pray

Action with purpose and calm achievement
lies at the heart of the universe;
quiet, creative, powerful and loving,
giving confidence, generosity, gentleness and care.
To know the energies of God,
to be sustained in his peace,
to receive the harvest of his sovereign rule,
we must go deep into God and deep into ourselves.
We need to refuse what is only surface
and look for the consonances beneath,
which hold together divine and human
and make them one.

Psalm

I will hear what the Lord God will speak:
> for he will speak peace to his people,
> > to his faithful ones, whose hearts are turned to him.
Truly his salvation is near to those that fear him:
> and his glory shall dwell in our land.
Mercy and truth are met together:

righteousness and peace have kissed each other;
Truth shall flourish out of the earth:
    and righteousness shall look down from heaven.
The Lord will also give us all that is good:
    and our land shall yield its plenty.
For righteousness shall go before him:
    and tread the path before his feet.

Psalm 85:8–13

Bible reading

On the evening of that day, the first day of the week, the doors being shut where the disciples were, for fear of the Jews, Jesus came and stood among them and said to them, 'Peace be with you.' When he had said this he showed them his hands and his side. Then the disciples were glad when they saw the Lord. Jesus said to them again, 'Peace be with you. As the Father has sent me, even so I send you.'

John 20:19–21

(Additional readings: Isaiah 55:10–13; Romans 8:31–39 or 12:14–21.)

Song

Risen Jesus,
we thank you for your greeting,
'Peace be with you.'
The shalom of God, deep lasting peace;
peace that brings inner calm;
and keeps a person steady in the storm;
that faces the persecutor without fear
and proclaims the good news with courage and with joy.
This is the peace that reconciles

sister to brother, black to white,
rich and poor, young and old;
but not a peace that is quiet
in the face of oppression and injustice.
This is peace with God,
the peace that passes understanding.

John Johansen-Berg

Prayer

Even in the dark night of peoples, there are those who keep alive the flickering flame. From humble prayer, they draw the freedom to resist harsh turmoil, their souls lifted high with hope. When tirelessly it listens and heals, when it lives out reconciliation, the Church becomes what is most luminous about it: the limpid reflection of a love.

Brother Roger of Taizé

Find three or four stones or pebbles, and begin by holding one in each hand, leaving the others aside. Notice the shapes of the two stones and the differences between them. Begin to look for ways in which they might fit together.

Then place the stones in front of you and consider the variety of human life which God has created and which is constantly seeking to resolve its disharmony into a unity. Allow the images you are creating to illuminate the conflict and the longings for peace which exist among the people you know, and pray for them.

Ask God to touch you with his peace – deep peace, running over into all the world around – and ask him to reveal his way of reconciliation, healing and wholeness.

Draw together all the stones and fit them into various patterns – sometimes out of step together, hard and harsh, and sometimes finding a harmony and satisfying shape where each plays its part to make a new and better shape than any one stone can have on its own. Then turn to God and ask him to bring to the world his harmony and peace.

Prayer

Father and God,
we constantly break up the world you have given us
through our habitual violence, selfishness and sin;
easily and thoughtlessly we make entrances for evil
without considering the dangers and horror
of its destructive power;
and we pay no heed to the cost to others
of our terrible deeds:
forgive us,
and restore us to the place of your peace;
bring all people together in your love;
and teach us the path to righteousness and joy.

Meditations

Not as the world gives

Jesus has many followers; and also many admirers who respond to the Everest-like challenge of his moral vision. For instance, one of his sayings from the Beatitudes is treasured by people of all religions and none: 'How blest are the peacemakers; God shall call them his sons' (Matt. 5:9). These words of promise and hope give never-ending inspiration to humanity's search for peace, a longing which Jesus clearly knew for himself. However, because any peace built by humanity is intolerably fragile, little more than a stack of cards, the frustration of peacemaking remains as unending as the search.

Jesus also knew how peace can never be achieved while the longing for it remains vague and sentimental. The passion of desire must be combined with the skill of astute thought and sustained effort. Humanity's peace has to be constructed, promoted, vigilantly preserved and eagerly shared. Law, treaty, custom, even courtesy and manners are all, in various ways, building-blocks used by every community to cultivate peace and mutual well-being, for the good and proper functioning of society.

Sometimes we look for a peace which can never be, partly because we misconceive both what we are looking for and how it might come about.[16] Jesus was nurtured on the traditional Jewish vision of peace summed up in Micah 4:1–4, which contains both a vision of peace and the method to bring it into being. Micah says those who come to God and his judgement find a stable, secure environment in which they can prosper, have work and rest, and achieve fulfilment. The biblical promise of peace is offered to all who accept God's sovereignty, regardless of their origins, their religion or their culture, and one major purpose of Jesus' preaching is to bring those who hear the ancient message to the moment of saving grace. Jesus proclaims God to be Saviour precisely because he establishes and makes permanent harmony between people, ridding the world of conflict and replacing it with peace.

After Easter Jesus' greeting to his friends is always 'Peace be with you.' Before his death Jesus had said to them, 'Peace is my parting gift to you, my own peace, such as the world cannot give' (John 14:27), but significantly, they had to wait until after Easter to receive his gift. By his death and resurrection Jesus brought into being a new order of creation in which the human search for peace touches and becomes the costly road to the Father's kingdom; a road which Jesus accepted for himself and which he knew his friends would also have to take. 'The hour is coming, has indeed already come, when you are all to be scattered, each to his home, leaving me alone. Yet I am not alone, because the Father is with me. I have told you all this so that in me you may find peace. In the world you will have trouble. But courage! The victory is mine; I have conquered the world' (John 16:31–33).

Christians, following Jesus, know at least two dimensions of peace. One is the kind of peace which it is our duty to construct and preserve and the other is the peace which is God-given, and which can only be received if we are prepared to go the Way of the Cross. Although we can distinguish between the two, there is no sharp wedge separating them, and in any deep and persistent pursuit of peace both flow together and reinforce each other. We seek both: peace built on the justice to which all human beings must commit themselves, and peace given and received – given by God when we are brought to him by Jesus in the power of resurrection and received when our discipleship is a costly offering of self to God in praise and to others in their need.

> Lord Jesus,
> you called your friends
> to be for all people
> makers and bringers of peace.
> Open our ears to your greeting of
> 'Peace.'
> Stop us being dreamers only
> and enable us to be
> signs in the world
> of the peace and hope
> to which all created beings are called.

Give us your strength
to bear in ourselves
the suffering and the peacemaking
which you promise
are the birth-pain of the Father's kingdom.

Scar-tissue and wounds of glory

Kate Boljan was aged twenty-two and was eight months pregnant when she and her husband Ante were trapped during the war in the beautiful holiday resort of Dubrovnik. She told Alan Little, a BBC correspondent, how she had to decide whether to stay or leave on the last refugee ship, choosing between her husband and her unborn child. 'I don't know whether I will see him again, or whether he will see the child. My baby will need water and food and electricity. Of course it was a hard decision.' Kate and her child and her husband, whether they meet again or not, may be only one family in millions who have suffered in this way, but they will carry the scars of their experience for the rest of their lives.

Moving through life, few people avoid deep scarring. We receive endless mental, as well as physical wounds, and the healing process is complex and takes for ever. St Paul once said of the scars he had received: 'I bear in my body the marks of the Lord Jesus' (Gal. 6:17). Probably he had been told that when Jesus was with the disciples again after Easter he had shown them the marks of the nails and spear which had entered his flesh and were still with him. The surprise is to read in the Gospel that the sight of Jesus' wounds brought joy to his friends.

There were perhaps two reasons for this. First, seeing the wounds from Jesus' physical body still present in his risen body assured the disciples that he was the same person before and after Calvary. The ever-visible scars affirm that 'Jesus Christ is the same yesterday, today, and for ever' (Heb. 13:8). Now he is with us all through our lives, whatever happens to us, as he promised. He is to be 'worshipped, trusted and adored', as we often sing.

Another reason is that by seeing Jesus' wounds the disciples recognized and believed in the continuity between the man they had been with and the risen Lord they were with now. The presence of Jesus with his life renewed is a sign, from within the kingdom in its fullness and now from within the world even in its incompleteness, that God's healing processes cannot be thwarted. There will always be pain, but the healing which comes through and with it will be thorough and complete. 'I reckon that the sufferings we now endure,' wrote St Paul, 'bear no comparison with the splendour, as yet unrevealed, which is in store for us' (Rom. 8:18).

Christians train themselves to identify their own scarring and unnumbered wounds with their discipleship. Not an easy thing to do, and not a claim to be made without deep thought and reflection, or else the badge of membership is trivialized and made a nonsense. New health and fulfilled life come through the process of being born into the divine kingdom, which is our resurrection and which we begin to experience here and now. However costly the sacrifice seems at times – we might even want to dismiss it as unreasonable – the calculation we make is not the pain we endure but the joy which comes through bearing it.

Easter joy is rooted in facts – the fact of Jesus' death and resurrection, the fact that his followers share this baptism of pain and joy, and the fact that many experience for themselves real life being transfigured by God's love and forgiveness. In the risen Christ the divine creative energy is present among us with a quiet and irreversible power over evil of

every kind, giving us now the chance to gather a harvest of
peace.

Father.
you know the suffering of all your sons and daughters,
you know the suffering endured in body and mind
in your dearly loved Son,
Jesus our Lord.
Constantly you bear all human suffering
in your divine heart and being:
when we are scarred and torn,
hold our wounds close enough to you,
that your promised glory
may rise within us,
to shine before all the world,
for ever.

Sixth Week of Easter
and Ascension

Praise, honour and glory

Beginning to pray

Caught and carried by the wind, a kite flies up;
By the energy and action of wings, the lark ascends;
When excitement stirs our spirit, we are roused.
All touch the power of God,
Who breathes into his creation his Spirit of life,
And we glimpse the triumph of goodness
Which can never end,
And which with confidence and great joy
We celebrate today and for ever.
Alleluia!

Psalm

O worship the Lord in the beauty of his holiness:
    let the whole earth stand in awe of him.
Say among the nations that the Lord is king:
    he has made the world so firm
        that it can never be moved;
        and he shall judge the peoples with equity.

Let the heavens rejoice and let the earth be glad:
    let the sea roar, and all that fills it:
Let the fields rejoice, and everything in them:
    then shall all the trees of the wood
        shout with joy before the Lord;
For he comes, he comes to judge the earth:
    he shall judge the world with righteousness,
        and the peoples with his truth.

Psalm 96:9–13

Bible reading

When they were all together, the disciples asked Jesus, 'Lord, is this the time when you are to establish once again the sovereignty of Israel?' He answered, 'It is not for you to know about dates or times, which the Father has set within his own control. But you will receive power when the Holy Spirit comes upon you; and you will bear witness for me in Jerusalem, and all over Judaea and Samaria, and away to the ends of the earth.' When he had said this, as they watched, he was lifted up, and a cloud removed him from their sight.

Acts 1:6–9

(Additional readings: Luke 24:44–53; Ephesians 4:7–16; Isaiah 65:17–19.)

Song

Let joy break out, eternal God!
Take the self-imposed blindfold from our eyes,
Rob us of the crutches we so dearly love.
Unshackle mind and heart,
And grant the freedom you have ever planned.

Let joy break out!
Throw open wide the gate to life
and help us find ourselves.
Let joy break out!
and flood our lives;
    creation spilling out its brilliant gifts,
    love finding itself lost in love,
    silence deepened, and all sound enhanced.
Let joy break out! And break again!
    as your fatherly love enfolds us
    as Jesus speaks the intimate Word
    and the spirit enlivens our half-deadened lives.
Let joy break out! And joy again!

                            Donald Hilton

Prayer

All who listen, by day as well as in the watches of the night, all who welcome the gifts of the Holy Spirit, will discover that with almost nothing they have everything.
                              Brother Roger of Taizé

Explore the feelings of praise and joy which the images of Jesus as universal king attempt to picture and describe.

Look at whatever moves you to amazement and wonder. Think of the people who have enabled you to experience love and adoration. Thank God for them and all they have opened up for you. Ask him to enrich and fulfil this knowledge, and bring it into touch with his purposes for all his creation.

Consider how shallow and hollow so many things become alongside the glory of God. Reset your perspectives. Allow yourself to become more detached from them and more attached to the things which last for ever.

Prayer

> Holy Lord Jesus,
> radiant, exalted and beautiful,
> King of the nations
> yet without crown or earthly power:
> you give yourself to all people
> that they may come to God.
> Be with us now,
> that knowing only his praise and glory,
> we may be drawn
> closer to his heart and will
> and stand within his kingdom
> which alone lasts for ever.

Meditations

Emotion and achievement

In his autobiography *Surprised by Joy*, C. S. Lewis wrote movingly about how he grew in spirit, in prayer and devotion once he realized that some beliefs are difficult not because they are hard to understand but because they are hard to imagine. 'Very often the inability to believe is not a failure of the intellect but a failure of the imagination,' he says.

The great festival of the ascension, when we try to describe the moment of final victory for the risen Jesus, definitely taxes human imagination to the full. No, literally he did not just go up and up. Not even the New Testament says he did. On the mountainside, St Luke describes a cloud which received Jesus, obscured him and took him from the sight of the disciples. Anyone who knows the Bible, especially the Old Testament, as the disciples did, knows that in their tradition a cloud represents the presence of God. St Luke is saying that

Jesus, no longer visible, is taken into the full presence of God. Thus he proclaims that now Jesus is with God, with his Father, held in the divine love. A fact which Christians believe, but a fact which is hard to imagine.

By receiving Jesus into the glory of his abiding presence God gives him what we might well call his seal of approval. At the time of Jesus' baptism by John, the divine voice proclaimed and prophesied, 'This is my beloved Son with whom I am well pleased' (Matt. 3:17). Jesus is the one in whom God delights, and those who are truly with Jesus – incorporated into him, as we say (using words accurately), to be his brothers and sisters – are also at-one-with God and give him further joy. Together with Jesus they too receive God's welcome and unreserved approval. In Christ, they also look forward to hearing words of praise: 'Well done, good and faithful servant. You have been faithful over a little. I will set you over much. Enter into the joy of your Master' (Matt. 25:21).

The word 'ascension' intellectually is far from straightforward, of course, primarily because we no longer accept a three-decker sense of 'going up' or believe that 'heaven' (the place where God is) is above the bright blue skies. Some help is offered, though, when we remember that the ascension of Jesus is first and foremost an affirmation of what we already believe, rather than an extra belief, separate and detachable from what surrounds it and tacked on at the end. It is a further and deeper exploration of Easter and is a matter of filling out, making a further discovery in meaning; it is a matter of imagination *before* it is anything else. To put it rather dramatically and to use a Bible image, if we believe the resurrection and cannot believe the ascension, then we are swallowing a camel and straining at a gnat.

How to picture this aspect of divine achievement then will always be a struggle, but the celebration, enjoyment and appreciation of the fact does not depend on any spatial analogy we use to illustrate it being 'literally true', nor does accepting pictures and symbols exactly for what they are invalidate or change the fact to which we assent.

Any climber who actually gets to the peak is bound to be filled with exhaustion and exhilaration. For instance, when Rebecca Stephens climbed Everest in 1993 the headlines in the press used her own words: 'I'm on top of the world!' Perhaps such an image helps. Emotions and achievement came together for her in a burst of triumph.

That is the Festival of Ascensiontide: the actual fact that in Christ aspiration and reality, emotion and achievement combine in a burst of triumph.

> Risen and ascended Lord,
> open our hearts and minds to see the fullness of your glory,
> won through pain and suffering
> and given by the Father in his great love.
> Help us to stretch imagination and reason
> as far as we can make them go,
> to recognize wonder and awe,
> to celebrate and enjoy the signs of glory
> in every part of creation,
> leading to praise and adoration.
> Alleluia!

Where Christ has gone before

Apparently to climb Everest nowadays is almost an ordinary affair. There is even a refuse problem on the mountain because so many do go for the top and get there, and they don't take their rubbish home with them! That too can help us picture better a further part of the meaning of the ascension. Not the rubbish, but the fact that once conquered, the mountain became easier for others to climb afterwards. Once it had happened others began to go the same way and achieve the same prize.

They say the first tenor to sing a top B flat (normally the highest note a tenor can reach) burst a blood vessel in the process, collapsed and didn't survive. Now, because it was done once, Pavarotti and any tenor worth his salt will sing that top note like a canary. In similar vein the Jews tell an old story about the Exodus. They say it wasn't until one person dared to take the plunge and jump into the sea that the waters finally parted. We sing of what Jesus achieved in his ascension:

> There was no other good enough
> > To pay the price of sin;
> He only could unlock the gate
> > Of heaven and let us in.

Each of these examples points in the same direction. Jesus has opened up a way ahead for us which now, in his company and strength, we can travel ourselves. The Westminster Confession in the seventeenth century defined our purpose in life as to be with God and to enjoy him for ever, and that enjoyment can be ours. Even within the limitations and sorrows of this world, those who are with Jesus can experience at least something of what it is like 'to ascend with him and with him continually dwell' in the eternal presence of God.

The real danger is not so much that we shall lose the meaning of Ascensiontide through our colander-like and inadequate images, but that we shall lose it by treating the festival as a diversion, an attempt to escape harsh reality. To prevent that happening, the ascension is firmly rooted in the cross. Jesus did not enter into his glory until he had gone to Calvary, despising the shame. Nor can we.

Some fifty years or more ago Evelyn Underhill wrote:

> We 'follow the footsteps of His most holy life' by treading the firm rough earth, up hill and down dale, on the mountain, by the lake-side, in garden, temple, street, or up the strait way to Calvary.

The kingdoms of this world are becoming the kingdom of Christ: slowly, so slowly and with many painful set-backs, and certainly not with any kind of triumphalism. But the victory of the gospel is substantial to those who carry their own cross and whatever part of the Cross of the World God is asking us to bear as well. The bubbling surfaces of happiness at Ascensiontide catch us up and carry us along fearlessly, so that we know and experience the sovereignty exercised by God over all his creation. We need not hold back from the joy, but we need to go forward also and enrol in the group of those who tackle the never-ending task of serving others in their increasingly desperate need. Ascension is about the going of the Son to the Father and about the coming of God's kingdom on earth as it is in heaven, and about the cost of that kingdom.

Through our praise and prayers, through the deep, well-founded joy of our hearts and minds, above all through the consecration and giving of self, we are brought to God by Jesus and experience for ourselves his triumph and glory.

Lord Jesus,
risen and ascended
Saviour and Christ:

help us to follow in your footsteps
which took you to the cross,
where too we must go
to find the path
to the glory of God.
Alleluia!

Seventh Week of Easter and Pentecost

Renewing the face of the earth

Beginning to pray

Spirit of God,
bringing all creation into being,
renewing and healing it
of the sharp brokenness of evil and sin;
bringing everything to the place of God's rule.
We hear you speak the music of his love
in wind, fire and water,
in stillness and silence.
Inspire us with your truth.
Support us with your tireless strength.
Love us, and set us free at last
to love you,
to love others,
and to love ourselves.

Psalm

When you hide your face, they are troubled:
    when you take away their breath,
        they die and return to their dust.
When you send forth your spirit they are created:
    and you renew the face of the earth.

May the glory of the Lord endure for ever:
>   may the Lord rejoice in his works.
If he look upon the earth, it shall tremble:
>   if he but touch the mountains, they shall smoke.
I will sing to the Lord as long as I live;
>   I will praise my God while I have any being.
May my meditation be pleasing to him:
>   for my joy shall be in the Lord.
May sinners perish from the earth,
>   let the wicked be no more:
bless the Lord, O my soul; O praise the Lord.

Psalm 104:29–35

Bible reading

While the day of Pentecost was running its course the disciples were all together in one place, when suddenly there came from the sky a noise like that of a strong driving wind, which filled the whole house where they were sitting. And there appeared to them tongues like flames of fire, dispersed among them and resting on each one. And they were filled with the Holy Spirit and began to talk in other tongues, as the Spirit gave them power.

Acts 2:1–4

(Additional readings: John 3:5–8; Romans 8:14–17; Joel 2:21–29.)

Song

God, you invite us to dance in delight,
shaping and forming in figures of grace.
We move to the pulse of creation's music
and rejoice to be part of the making of earth.

Praise in the making, the sharing, the moving;
praise to the God who dances with us.

In the steps of Jesus we reach to our partners,
touching and holding and finding our strengths.
Together we move into patterns of freedom,
and rejoice to be part of the sharing of hope.

Praise in the making, the sharing, the moving;
praise to the God who dances with us.

We whirl and spin in the Spirit's rhythm,
embracing the world with our circles of joy.
Together we dance for salvation and justice,
and rejoice to be part of the moving of love.

Praise in the making, the sharing, the moving;
praise to the God who dances with us.

Jan Berry

Prayer

Do you hear the Holy Spirit saying to you, 'I am familiar
with your trials and your poverty, yet you are filled to over-
flowing'? Filled by what? By the love of Christ, source of
freedom, hidden in the depths of your being.

Brother Roger of Taizé

Train yourself to listen –
which often means going through a process of
    being still,
    being empty of self and much else,
    becoming attentive to all that lies beyond and outside of
      us,
    noticing new thoughts,
    following them through patiently,
    without prejudice or pre-judgement.

Use the image of the dance to think of
    the creation of a circle of harmony
    which brings together your will and God's will,
    the moving together and the moving apart
    in partnership between yourself and God,
    the closeness, the distance,
    the diminishing gaps, the widening spaces,
    as the partnership changes
    and moves through the years of your life.

Ask God the Holy Spirit to breathe into you the refreshing newness of the joy, the freedom and the movement of his life within you.

Prayer

Holy Spirit of God,
for ever free to visit and flow
within every part of the Father's creation,
within every person held in his love:
fill us now with your energy;
heal us with your forgiveness;
strengthen and confirm us by the gifts
your graciousness is giving.
Let us treasure and use them to the full,
so that we may become
what we long to be,
and receive more and more of the joy
of the kingdom of heaven on earth.

Meditations

You will know the truth and the truth will set you free

Sydney Carter the hymn-writer has written:

> the kingdom of God is within: but you cannot get it out, excepting with the help of other people. By their otherness you dig to what is in yourself.

Pentecost is sometimes called the festival of freedom and liberation because it celebrates the power of God the Holy Spirit to release from within the person, made in the image of the Father, which is struggling to get out. We are all in one way or another 'unfinished people', like Shakespeare's Richard III, 'sent into this breathing world, scarce half made up'. Being born a second time, being renewed, becoming what we are meant to be, are all ways of describing the work of God the Holy Spirit within us, who is constantly at work, bringing us to wholeness, fulfilment and completion.

One of the headmasters I worked with was not too popular with his colleagues or his pupils. He wasn't actively disliked but no one was able to warm to him, as we say. But I remember one member of staff who agreed with the general opinion and then always added: 'Yes – but I feel there's a better person inside struggling to get out.' Like so many other people, that man was his own worst enemy, and sadly, he didn't much like other people helping him to find himself either.

Often we hinder our own better selves and turn away from the help which we could receive and which is so gladly offered. When we say God the Holy Spirit is leading us into truth we mean the capacity latent in every person to relate to the truth in such a way that it frees us and liberates us and promotes within us the conquest of that hollow 'living and partly living' [17] which too often holds us in its barren grasp.

Sydney Carter is right. We need both the power of the Holy Spirit and also the company of others to be as God would have us be. We need the Spirit-filled community (another name for the Church) because we are midwives to one another as we walk in the Spirit and make our journey from earth to heaven.

> In that One
> there is Another.
> In that I
> there is a You.
> Holy is the
> One forever.
> Holy is the
> Other too.
>
> Sydney Carter

Giving birth is being born[18]

Jesus promised to send the Spirit to the disciples to do two things – to guide and lead them into the truth, and to give them the strength they needed *to bear* the truth.

Ferreting out information, finding out the facts, collating and sifting the evidence – that is one way to find something of the truth, a way never to be underestimated and yet never to be overstated either. Possessing this knowledge, knowing the facts and having a passion for accuracy will help us pass exams, enable us to build bridges which will be strong enough to carry loads and not collapse under them, or perhaps help us to discriminate between heresy and orthodoxy. Human projects which are all worth the hard thought and energy put into them. But as we saw in the first meditation, that is not the truth Jesus means when he says to us, 'I will pray the Father, and he will send you another Comforter to be with you forever – even the Spirit of truth' (John 14:16–17). He means knowing truth in such a way that we are able to relate to ourselves, to others and to God in a fulfilling and satisfying way. Truth known in relationship is the source of harmony and unity.

Nowadays within the Church there is a great deal of dissension, as there is in society generally. It reveals how much strength we need if we are to bear the truth. They have a saying in the Netherlands: where there is a Dutchman there is a church, where there are two Dutchmen there is a division, and where there are three Dutchmen there is another church! Broken and fragmented churches are scattered across Christian history. Each time such a break occurs the power of the Holy Spirit is rejected and abandoned. Christian disunity is a sign to the Church and to the world that the Christian community is neither Spirit-filled nor Spirit-led. Constantly the Christian community needs healing.

Controversy is good if it gives us a passion for truth, but it is bad if it makes us behave towards each other with a less than Christian graciousness and acceptance. What should most concern us about any debate among Christians is not the matter of the argument but the method of the discussion. Whichever side of any controversy we are on, there is a first principle which all must accept. The vision of God is available only to those who seek holiness as well as knowledge. 'Blessed are the pure in heart for they shall see God' (Matt. 5:8). Christian behaviour has always had a priority over formal Christian believing; just as there were many Christians following the living Lord before any began to recite creeds.

Bearing the truth, which is more than knowing and living with it, is beyond our natural strength because ultimate truth confronts us with a reality of which human beings cannot bear very much. God in his love, though, never leaves us on our own nor asks us to bear anything beyond the combined capacity of our human nature and his divine grace. Jesus' prayer to the Father that we might be given another Comforter, one as strong for us as his own presence was to the disciples when they were with him in the flesh, has been answered. The Holy Spirit brings together nature and grace, unifying them and strengthening them within each person who is born of both flesh and Spirit and

… none can guess its grace,
Till he become the place
Wherein the Holy Spirit makes his dwelling.

Part Three
Easter People

To Christ the Seed
Ag Criost an siol

To Christ the seed, to Christ the crop,
in barn of Christ may we be brought.

To Christ the sea, to Christ the fish,
in nets of Christ may we be caught.

From growth to age, from age to death,
Thy two arms here, O Christ, about us.

From death to end – not end but growth –
in blessed Paradise may we be.

Ancient Irish prayer

Crowned with glory now

There was no cross cross enough
to nil me
to still me
I hung as gold that bled, and bloomed
A rose that rose and prised the tomb
away from Satan's wilful doom
There was no cross, death, grave
or room
to hold me.

Stewart Henderson

For several centuries and for various reasons the early
Christians did not observe a particular festival to commemo-
rate the crucifixion of Jesus, partly because they could not
make the death of their hero into a public celebration in
Roman society because he had been condemned, however
unjustly, as a criminal; and partly because, more than
anything else, they wanted to celebrate life in Christ, which
they did in the great liturgy held on the night of Easter. Doing
without a yearly Good Friday was not the deprivation it
sounds. For them the cross was simply not the starting point
for faith anyway. Their faith was based entirely on the experience of Easter into which they had been baptized.[19] Every day
they lived what we might call 'resurrection-life' in the here
and now. The message they proclaimed was 'Jesus lives!', and
the regular Eucharist, the act of thanksgiving using bread and

wine made at the start of each week, was the sign to them, and to any who could recognize it, of the continuing and abiding presence of the risen Lord with them, inspiring and empowering them.

Christians celebrated the first day of the week because with the resurrection of Jesus it had become 'the eighth day', the first day of the Age to Come, in the New World – the time of what happens *after* God's rest on 'the seventh day', the time of the last and greatest act of divine creativity, when his final and complete sovereignty had arrived and was beginning to work in the world, like yeast, spreading in all its depth and power. A time which would always be present tense and have no end; a time and activity in which Jesus had participated while he was alive on earth, and the secret of which he had revealed in advance through his ministry of preaching and healing to those with ears to hear and eyes to see and a willingness to follow; a time which even while it remains part of historical calculation yet has the status of eternity.

Although at this period in the history of the Church there was no Good Friday to be separated from the Easter festival,[20] this does not mean the first Christians did not know the details of what happened at Calvary or disregarded them. They had to guard against trivializing their commitment to the Easter Faith and allowing it to become shallow and escapist. Constantly they explored their faith in the resurrection further to enrich and deepen it, which inevitably meant confronting the events of Jesus' suffering and death.

There is always the danger that those who know the joy of the kingdom will underestimate the cost of the kingdom; and there is always the possibility that they will underestimate the significance of Jesus' death, the full extent of its pain and horror, and the terrible cost to both God and humankind which it spells out so clearly. Certainly in the preaching of the early Church the killing of Jesus is never left out (e.g. Acts 2:23ff; 3:15ff), and St Paul developed a detailed theology of the cross and the death of Christ to show what it reveals of the ways of God, which are always 'strange' to us (Isa. 55:8–9) and which require explanation. Eventually the four Gospels were written, and as we said in the meditations, they are best described as 'passion narratives with extended introductions'.

Yet when Christians live as Easter People and look more carefully at the death of Jesus and wrestle with its meaning, they are not taking a backward glance or giving in to a morbid curiosity or even at first making an historical enquiry. Primarily they are searching for the source of the new life they are enjoying. For our purposes now, we want to emphasize that the source of all Christian insight into the cross comes from an exploration of existing Easter Faith rather than an examination of human evil and what happened at Calvary. Like St Paul, Christians should begin any exploration of the cross by thinking through their own encounters and meetings with the risen Lord and then considering the consequence, which is life lived eucharistically in thanksgiving and service.

> If Christ was not raised, then our gospel is null and void, and so is your faith; and we turn out to be lying witnesses for God, because we bore witness that he raised Christ to life ... the truth is, Christ was raised to life – the firstfruits of the harvest (1 Cor. 15:14–15, 20).

Easter is not the contradiction or reversal of Good Friday. We could explore the facts surrounding the death of Jesus (though not in New Testament terms, admittedly) without necessarily reaching any understanding of Easter. There is

nothing in Good Friday which inevitably takes us on to Easter
Day and links the one and the other. A consideration of the
events of Jesus' suffering, trial and death does not automati-
cally produce a resurrection faith. But turn things the other
way round, and there is an inevitable link between Easter and
Good Friday. Here we cannot have the one without the other.
Easter without Good Friday is, in the end, a mirage, an
empty, rootless half-truth.

Good Friday therefore illuminates Easter rather than the
other way round. Each time we return to the central Christian
experience of knowing the risen Lord we find ourselves going
deeper into the fact, recorded in the fourth Gospel, that Jesus'
risen body still bears the wounds of his suffering and the
marks of his dying (John 20:19–29). The approach to Good
Friday which we used in the meditations and prayers began
with a firm belief that the extent to which we are grasping the
Easter Faith, being held by it and growing in it, determines
how much we can get to grips with the awful truth about the
crucifixion, and how far we can become part of it and take in
the details of what happens whenever evil attempts to destroy
the good.

This may well come as a surprise. Surely the more we are
'baptized into Jesus' death' the more we find out what it is to
be 'raised with him' (cf. Rom. 6:3–11). Yes, but St Paul was
speaking of what he experienced *after* he had encountered
the Risen Jesus on the Damascus Road. He described an
experience of spiritual growth while he lived with his faith in
the resurrection. Quite deliberately God structures the experience of discipleship and illumination so that the more we
know the presence of Jesus risen, the more we are able to
understand the appalling facts of his death and see them as
the final victory over the powers which fight against God's
kingdom. Father Neville Figgis of the Community of the

Resurrection at Mirfield used to say: 'Christ's rising is less a wonder than his dying – *if he be who he is.*'[21]

A great New Testament scholar, Edwyn Hoskyns, in his teaching earlier this century tried to start in the same place with his students and hold together what originally early Christian devotion and liturgy had kept together. He tried to work out both the theology and the ethics of early Christianity by forging a new word, Crucifixion-Resurrection,[22] which he refused to break down into its two parts. We can readily admit that it is difficult to hold the ideas together as a single concept. For many centuries, both in prayer and thought, the experience of Jesus' resurrection and death has been examined by Christians under its two principal headings rather than being held together as a unity. The danger in considering the parts rather than the whole, though, is that we may start in the wrong place, and by finding the secondary meaning miss the primary meaning.

To begin with the cross and do our best to work forwards to the resurrection, as we are often tempted to do, never takes us far enough. Only God can create life renewed and fulfilled in the resurrection, and it has to be received entirely as his gift, his gift of grace, freely and unconditionally given to those whom Christ brings to his Father with him.

> There are many dwelling-places in my Father's house; if it were not so I should have told you; for I am going there on purpose to prepare a place for you. And if I go and prepare a place for you, I shall come again and receive you to myself, so that where I am you may be also (John 14:2–4).

Those who begin with Good Friday instead of Easter will find the good news they are trying to hear and receive badly distorted, probably without realizing the full implications of

why and what they are doing.[23] Such an approach not only
ignores and reverses the experience of faith known to the
earliest Christian witnesses but it also leads to mistakes and
misconceptions, and takes us into a cul-de-sac which ought to
have a 'No entry' sign over it. It is simply the wrong way
round to tell the truth or the story. After all, when the Friday
fast, three days before Easter Day, became the day of the
commemoration of the cross and death of Jesus, from the
start the day was called 'Good', which clearly implies that it
was already understood in the knowledge of Easter.

There is another reason why a back-to-front approach is
dangerous. The gospel which Christians invite the world to
celebrate is about how good overcomes evil (Rom. 12:21).
The purpose of preaching and announcing the 'good news' of
this victory to a world still held in the grip of evil is to enable
each person to face up to and undergo the particular
encounter with evil which they have to bear at any moment,
in whatever form it takes. 'In the world you will have trouble.
But courage! The victory is mine; I have conquered the world'
(John 16:33).

Put this message the wrong way round, and it looks less
like news – good, bad or indifferent – and more like a smoke-
screen which attempts to disguise evil or minimize its impact,
or pretend it doesn't exist – a confidence-trick which is
quickly seen through and dismissed for what it is. Bishop
Kallistos Ware clearly sets the proper perspective when he
describes God's Easter gift to us as 'a joy-creating sorrow': a
gift without price for those held in the grip of evil.

As far as they can, Christians should never try to understand evil or ask the all-too-familiar question 'Why?' without
already holding and being held by a reliable anchor, a 'sure
and certain hope'. Whenever possible we should look at evil
with hope based firmly on God's achievement, revealed by

resurrection, rather than with a fragile human desire that things might be better or different from what they are. To look at the cross without a knowledge of Easter (which is actually an impossibility now, even if personal experience of resurrection is as yet withheld) would be to face an abyss from such a giddying height that it would be bound to produce acute despair.

Usually any way of handling evil we manage to bring together from solely human resources simply accommodates it in some way or another to the limitations of our starting point – the little faith, if any, which we have. In such a weakened condition we have to shelter from the full blast of the terrible truth.[24] Freud, following Marx, said 'religion is the opium of the masses', in which he may well have been oversimplifying, but he also said 'religion remains at the heart of a heartless world', about which he was right – unless the gospel is true and until discipleship reveals *how* good overcomes evil; that is, unless and until we have reason to know that we do not live in a heartless world but in a world created and held secure by the heart and love of a faithful Creator (Ezek. 36:24–30).

If Christians are ever to discover an adequate way of handling evil, let alone 'explaining' it, they must pay attention to its context as well as its nature. Often nowadays, when there is so much evil and violence shown in films, on TV screens and reported in graphic detail in the media, rightly we complain and say how dangerous this daily diet has become. Evil destroys by feeding on itself and sucking into itself everything it can. Many are gradually being destroyed by having to face unending reports of hard violence and torture of every kind. To steady our nerve, commentators claim this is nothing new. They point out how much violence there is in Greek tragedy and the plays of Shakespeare. But that is glib nonsense and misses an all-important point. The violence in Shakespeare's plays, however brutal and bestial, is always placed alongside great grandeur and nobility. In other words, it is violence held within a context: the worse and the worst are held in the context of the better and the best. Given that starting point, the perspective from which we look at the horror and tragedy which faces us changes significantly. Alongside the reality of evil we are offered a way to grapple with the truth about human suffering and evil without losing touch with hope. The imbalance in many films and TV dramas is the real danger; perhaps even more than the inclusion of violence, though that has reached appalling proportions of whose effect we are only dimly becoming aware. We need to take seriously the danger we create when evil is presented and considered without the hope of the gospel, without a belief that in Jesus God has overcome it or, if such a gospel cannot be accepted yet, at least some positive belief which holds the negative within it.

Unexpectedly, perhaps we need an entry-point into any examination of human evil which establishes a creative framework beforehand, not in an attempt to avoid the truth but to help receive it. I am convinced that because the extent to which we have an Easter Faith determines how much of the suffering and death of Jesus we can contemplate and take in, it also determines how much of the truth and the tragedy of the human condition we can face. Without a firm-based confidence, and an experience of living which reveals how good is overcoming evil, we shall hide from most of the facts and stand dead before them. I suspect it is the widespread weakness of any contemporary faith in the resurrection and our diminishing confidence in any belief that life is good and the universe can be trusted which seriously hinders our ability to recognize the nature of evil and handle it.

Nearly everyone speaks of 'the problem of evil', but there is too, if you like, 'a problem of good' which also structures human experience. The message is that good has overcome evil, and our experience of all that is good adds considerably to our confidence in that victory (Phil. 4:8). Christians look into the heart of darkness with the help of a light which enables them to celebrate and to hope in the teeth of the evilness of evil. Someone once said there is a choice facing the human race – between belief in God or suicide. I think we can see more clearly than ever what was meant. Without a reason to hope and the beginnings of an understanding of the victory of good over evil, we cannot attempt to deal with any evil without losing our nerve and becoming suicidal.

To help, Christian praise and devotion, and indeed theology, could be taken more like a pendulum rather than a straight forward-moving line. Whatever it is we are considering, we should start with Easter and the confidence, the hope and the demands which that experience brings. Then, exploring the experience as fully as possible, we shall find ourselves going back to take into account the events of Good Friday and what led up to it, which in turn will lead us forward again to include the concept of ascension and the giving of the Spirit. Celebrating and pondering whatever experience of Easter we have, making sense of it and coming to terms with its reality and depths, we move further and further backwards and further and further forwards to gather more and more into it. For example – moving backwards, we find ourselves experiencing penitence, suffering and loss, and then, swinging to the other end of the arc, we shall find forgiveness, receiving and gain, and all will be held in place by the central fact of the resurrection-life given by God to Jesus and to any who follow him and become his friends. Christians are an Easter People and 'Alleluia!' is their song.

To them the cross, with all its shame,
    With all its grace is given:
Their name an everlasting name,
    Their joy the joy of heaven.

They suffer with their Lord below,
    They reign with him above,
Their profit and their joy to know
    The mystery of his love.

The cross he bore is life and health,
    Though shame and death to him;
His people's hope, his people's wealth,
    Their everlasting theme.

                    Thomas Kelly (1769–1854)

The evilness of evil

Jesus Christ is in agony to the end of the world.

Blaise Pascal

Actors sometimes say it is easier to play bad rather than good characters. Perhaps there is more drama and energy in such parts, or at least the characteristics of moral failure are easier to communicate and more quickly recognized by an audience.[25] There is a definite attraction in such people, and at times we have for them a mixture of envy and misplaced admiration. Perhaps you too were one of those who wrote the famous school essay about the hero in Milton's *Paradise Lost*: is it God or Satan? Evil can fascinate us; more often it terrifies us and usually appears to have the upper hand (cf. Psalm 73). Evil in some shape or form is also clearly unavoidable for every human being, and for many people, whether believers or non-believers, how and why evil came to be and who, if anyone, is responsible for it remains for much of the time baffling and unanswerable.

> You can blame it onto Adam,
> You can blame it onto Eve,
> You can blame it on the Apple,
> But that I can't believe.
>
> You can blame it onto Pilate,
> You can blame it on the Jews,

You can blame it on the Devil,
It's God I accuse.

Sydney Carter ('It was on a Friday morning')

Speaking from his own personal experience, St Augustine recommended that when we are confronted by evil, instead of looking for someone to blame, we should cleave to God and try to discover that (a) all things he has made are good, (b) good is always capable of corruption, and (c) to reach any understanding of God's creation we must look at the whole rather than its parts: 'I no longer wished individual things to be better,' he writes, 'because I considered the totality.'[26] As we saw in the previous section, this is certainly a proper approach and likely to be both creative and productive. If we are to handle evil without being mesmerized or devoured by it, we must keep hold of a positive approach as far as we can and look at it with the eye of faith.

When theologians try to construct 'answers' to 'the problem of evil' they usually do so in the conviction that

> the justification for this world and its evils is to be found in its purpose – in the consequences it has for the souls of the persons in it. Actions and events make the world worse as they retard the process of soul-making, and they make the world better to the extent that they facilitate that purpose.[27]

To quote St Augustine again:

> [God] judged it better and more in accord with his power to bring some greater good out of evil than to permit no evil whatsoever.[28] ... If human nature should choose to fall away from God, misery proportionate to the offence was

bound to follow. Here, too, God foresaw the fall, the disregard of his law, the desertion from God, yet he left man's free choice unchecked because he also foresaw to what good he would turn man's evil.[29]

This concept of soul-making, though, as a justification for the existence of evil and the suffering of humanity in a divinely created world has always been debatable. It begs a question which in our time has become close to intolerable because of the unspeakable evils which regularly confront us. To double the agony we are immediately informed about them by the modern media, not always with as much sensitivity and responsibility as they need, with the result that all but the most hardened are very painfully and relentlessly absorbed into them. Even if we can see some aspects of individual growth coming through suffering patiently accepted, after the example of Christ, and even if like St Paul we see personal suffering making up the sufferings of Christ (Phil. 3:10), we are bound to ask, especially with the specific agony of the twentieth century in mind, does the end justify the means?

Some feel strongly in the depths of their being that it does not. They cannot believe soul-making at such huge cost is acceptable. They reject any kind of rational or theological framework which might be put round evil and the affliction it causes in an attempt to accommodate and explain it. Rarely does such a framework take seriously enough the sheer evilness of evil, which can no longer be contained within the traditional explanations which have been offered in the development of Christian thought.

Recently at least one theologian has warned that such attempts to explain and justify evil in the world viciously affront its victims. They make more intolerable the awfulness of the inferno that has to be endured. To suggest or hint that, in the end, all bad things are really 'good' and behind every evil there is 'an ultimate good' is dehumanizing and harmful simply because that is not the way in which such things are true, if indeed they are ever true.[30]

Rabbi Harold Kushner watched his son die of rapid ageing disease and said:

> I am a more sensitive person, a more effective pastor, a more sympathetic counsellor because of Aaron's life and death than I would ever have been without it. And I would give up all of those gains in a second if I could have my son back. If I could choose, I would forego all the spiritual growth and depth which has come my way because of our experience, and be what I was fifteen years ago, an average rabbi, an indifferent counsellor, helping some people and unable to help others, and the father of a bright, happy boy. But I cannot choose.[31]

A victim of the Holocaust goes even deeper:

> Never shall I forget that smoke.
> Never shall I forget the little faces of the children
>   whose bodies I saw turned into wreaths of smoke
>   beneath the silent blue sky.
> Never shall I forget those flames that consumed my faith
>   for ever.
> Never shall I forget that nocturnal silence
>   which deprived me for all eternity of the desire to
>   live.
> Never shall I forget those moments
>   which murdered my God and my soul
>   and turned my dreams to dust.

Never shall I forget these things, even if I am condemned
    to live as long as God himself.
Never.

People simply cannot follow St Augustine and use his talk
about God, such 'theology'. They find the appalling nature of
the parts outweighs any possible good which might be
produced by the whole. They ask how can any result or
purpose be proportionate in the face of ultimate and horrifying experiences like Rwanda, Cambodia, Bosnia, Dunblane
and above all the Holocaust. Moral human beings with the
smallest sense of justice must reject the proffered explanations because in the circumstances they are literally outra-
geous. To adapt Dylan Thomas' verse, all we can do is to
'Rage, rage, against the dying of the light.' [32]

Rationalizations offered by theology, philosophy, and some
human testimony easily obscure the full force of the evilness
of evil and allow us to turn away from it instead of
confronting it. [33] Only facing into the storm and somehow
coping with the situation in its full horror will do, and permit
human beings to retain any kind of dignity and integrity.

Inevitably, whenever there is a tragedy or disaster people
seek reasons. We see the cards tied to flowers of remembrance
with the word 'Why?' written on them, implying that (a)
there is an answer if only we could fathom it and (b) God
wouldn't have 'allowed' it to happen if he had been there: so
where was God when it happened? Such agony appears to
'prove' either that he is unable to help and succour human
beings in their deepest needs or that he doesn't care and
remains indifferent to 'the intolerable shirt of pain', [34] which
means he forfeits and cancels out any relationship we might
be inclined to develop with him. But we need to push through
and away from that first framework into which we fit our

thinking about suffering. Any attempt to work within such a frame of thought is a struggle for both mind and heart because it does not actually correspond accurately or sufficiently with the experience and knowledge of God and ourselves revealed by Jesus. Using it leads to confusion rather than clarification.

Sheila Cassidy's testimony was that during suffering the question 'Why?' is more often asked by the observer, the bystander, the sympathizer and thinker than by the person undergoing the suffering.[35] That does not in itself make it an invalid question, but it does rob it of some of those dimensions which most disturb us.

Perhaps too, the theoretical question can be put in such a strident tone that it hides rather than opens up the truth. On the cross Jesus was heard to say, 'My God, my God, why hast thou forsaken me?', but it was not his whole response to the events engulfing him. Jesus had already said on another occasion, 'He that shall endure to the end shall be saved' (Matt. 10:22), teaching that in the midst of suffering endurance is as important a quality as understanding, and he demonstrates what he taught by putting it into practice in his own passion and death. St Paul showed the same quality of endurance in suffering when he wrote from prison, 'I can do all things in Christ who strengthens me' (Phil. 4:13), and though he suffered constantly what he called 'a thorn in the flesh', he believed God provided a way of escape and said to him, 'My grace is sufficient for you, for my power is made perfect in weakness' (2 Cor. 12:7–9).

The other side of the question which is asked when suffering is happening is 'Where is God?' Again, the formulaic pattern of this particular question is profoundly misconceived and obscures rather than reveals truth.

Rabbi Hugo Gryn, who died early in 1997, was a survivor

of the extermination camps in Nazi Germany. He used to say the question 'Where is God?' as it is usually asked in times of suffering, especially by those who are observers and not participants, is a 'cop-out'. He insisted that the real question should be 'Where is Man?' – meaning we should investigate as fearlessly and as persistently as possible the full extent of 'man's inhumanity to man' before we even begin to think about God in such terrible situations. Usually if we investigate the actions of the human beings involved, somewhere we come very close to finding out the cause of the agony, and we also see pretty clearly the solution – if only we can find the courage and the wisdom to accept it. Terrible events of suffering demand a continental shift in our understanding of our own humanity with all its folly and beauty, its frailty and potential, its pride, vanity and hypocrisy, and its longings and aspirations for good. Dehumanization at the hands of others causes human agony more than any so-called 'absence' of God from among us. The answer to 'Where is God?' is always that he is in the sufferer, in the situation, deliberately choosing not to stand outside it. He is never absent or staying his hand or remaining silent. He suffers too.

We are often overheard saying we would have organized things differently if we had created a universe. We would have designed another kind of reality with a different set of rules. We want a way to get the desired result without the cost, which, as we saw earlier, is at times truly appalling;[36] a cost we would be right to refuse to pay unless we are convinced that the Creator himself is fully involved in the same terrifying process. The purpose of reading the story of Abraham and Isaac (Gen. 22:1–19) at Matins on Good Friday is to strengthen and deepen the truth that he is.

Some people take exception to the story of the horrifying journey to Mount Moriah because they think of it only from

Isaac's point of view. The story does not tell of a boy betrayed by his father, but of a father who faces the agony of losing the son he had longed for and for whom he had waited so patiently, a father who is himself compromised and numbered with the agents of the boy's suffering and tragedy. Abraham's agony is a picture of the suffering of God while the divine life is held within his created order with all its pain and evil. Its message is that God suffers as any parent would suffer while his dearly beloved Son faces such torture, and that God continues to suffer whenever any of his children face agony and horror.

> God is love: and he enfoldeth
>   all the world in one embrace;
> with unfailing grasp he holdeth
>   every child of every race.
> And when human hearts are breaking
>   under sorrow's iron rod,
> then they find that self-same aching
>   deep within the heart of God.
>
> Timothy Rees (1874–1939)

A community of suffering

There blows a cold wind today, today,
The wind blows cold today.
Christ suffered his passion for man's salvation,
To keep the cold wind away.

Fifteenth-century English carol

In a poem by W. H. Auden, the martyr St Cecilia encourages those who suffer and says to them, 'O wear your tribulation like a rose.' [37] If suffering can be turned into a kind of emblem (and I realize this is a pretty big 'If'), then another way opens up for us to consider how God is present and at work in his world. Because of the death of Jesus, victim is alongside victim. Mysteriously, all who suffer know they belong together and are held together. Suffering becomes a sign of belonging – to Christ and the Father, and to humanity itself.

If, like St Paul, we are persuaded that God is in Christ reconciling the world to himself (2 Cor. 5:19) and that the sufferings inflicted on both God and man are somehow the means of that reconciliation, then, in a stunning way, suffering offers those who are immersed in it a remarkable equality with God. Not an equality to be snatched at or to be assumed as 'of right', but an equality received from God with which those who follow Jesus to the end are invested. If those who suffer can say, 'We belong to God and he belongs to us', they have a sign that the Old Testament promises about the restoration of God's people to his full care and protection have been achieved. 'They shall live under the shelter of my dwelling; I will become their God and they shall become my people' (Ezek. 37:27).

Simply to be with others in their suffering can often be the only pastoral care we are able to offer each other, and we should never underestimate its value and strength. To explore the experience of shared suffering is an illuminating starting point for thinking about the divine care which surrounds us. Jürgen Moltmann gives a good example of how far identification between fellow sufferers can go. He points to

> the strange fact that the Christ of the poor has always been the crucified Christ. What do they themselves see in him? They clearly do not find in his passion another 'poor devil' who had no better luck than they. Rather, they find in him the brother who put off his divine form and took on the form of a slave, to be with them and to love them. They find in him a God who does not torture them but becomes their brother and companion.[38]

Solidarity in suffering is a creative action, and unless we become part of it ourselves, recruited and involved, we can only guess how much it costs those undergoing it.[39] We may not say those who bear suffering are saved *by it* because suffering is never God's will for his creation,[40] but we can say they are being saved *in spite of it and carried through it* because God is always present and working within human suffering; and miraculously somehow bearing suffering also saves those who with compassion stand alongside and share it. The greatest wonder of all is that in God's time and in his way the same suffering heals and redeems those who look on as well, whether they deserve it or not.[41]

Jesus asks all who hear him to consider and think about his teaching and then go further, to go on and take up the cross and follow. He insisted that the only way to find out truth is to couple deeds with words, actions with thoughts (John 7:17),[42] and as we saw in the meditations, he urges disciples not even to rely on the cross he carried but to find the meaning and enjoy the truth he knew by carrying their own cross, whatever form and shape it takes.

Another opportunity which solidarity in suffering brings is a way to explore truth from the inside rather than from the outside. The suggestion may sound odd to some nowadays because it appears too unscientific, too subjective to be reliable in a world where objectivity has the image of security and permanence. Yet, although we hear some scientists (fewer and fewer, incidentally) saying there is nothing beyond what we can apprehend with our senses, many say scientific observation and analysis can never be entirely objective. We are not misleading ourselves after all if we search for more truth in other ways. However marvellous are the gifts of science, we know how much they leave out, how many other things we need to sustain our humanity which they do and must overlook if they are to achieve their legitimately concentrated and limited goal.

A wholly objective enquirer into the passion and resurrection of Jesus will find it delivers up only part of its truth, which will not be the most significant or rewarding part. To know its other truth the enquirer must become part of the experience. There is truth to be worked at from within – discovered from the inside out. Suffering reveals truth which can be apprehended in no other way.[43]

Dennis Potter in his last interview with Melvyn Bragg said memorably, 'For me religion is the wound, not the bandage.'[44] However 'religious' we become, we remain part of the problem, not part of the solution. It sounds a hopeless state to be in. Yet all is not lost or impossibly circumscribed, because, as so many witnesses testify, God in his love is prepared to be in the same predicament with us.

> ... if the Bible is anything to go by, God is powerful *in the midst*. God is not an answer to particular questions, but is a constant resource, a constant experience, a constant promise in the midst of all these things.[45]

Surely God is almighty, omnipotent, able to work any miracle he please? How can he be weak, vulnerable, suffering? It seems to me that unless we can explain this, our faith is in vain, and we cannot tackle the main demand of the secular world today, which is to show, quite simply, that God exists. I say show, not prove, because anyone who expects the existence of God to be demonstrated by logic is playing at the wrong table. If it were possible to prove God logically, we would all have to become his slaves, which is not what a loving Father wants.

And so it came about that God's own Son – the ultimate sign of his love for us – was despised and rejected of men and nailed upon the cross by man's free will. And God was so weak that, his love being rejected, he could do nothing but hang there saying: 'I am like this: I am very like you.' He could do nothing but forgive – which is love, a form of love totally undeserved by those upon whom it is bestowed. Recognized, accepted and returned, it then becomes (as it has become) the mightiest power in the world: comforting, healing, pacifying, resurrecting – for never must we say the word crucifixion without resurrection.[46]

Gathering the promised fruit

Thou hast restored me again to the friendship of God, to the enjoyment of the world, to the hope of eternal glory, to the love of angels, cherubim and men, to the enjoyment and obedience of thy holy laws, which alone are sweeter to me than honey and the honeycomb, and more precious than thousands of gold and silver. Thou hast restored me above all to the image of God. O let thy love be in me, that thy joy may be fulfilled in me for evermore.

Thomas Traherne, *Centuries of Meditations*, 1–76

Near Hereford there are many outstanding examples of local Romanesque sculpture; among other places at Kilpeck and the great baptismal fonts at Eardisley and Castle Frome. In their art, the sculptors portrayed the nature of evil and the conflict which lies tangled up in the depths of the world which, as we have said in the previous section, we dare not underestimate either in its persistence or its destructive energy.

Romanesque art stands in the tradition of picturing God's struggle with evil as a battle and the universe as the battleground where it is fought out.[47] We said before that evil propagates by feeding on itself. The huge and menacing dragons which eat their own tails devour themselves, representing the corruption within the natural forces of life – fullness and harvest which by turning in on itself finally consumes itself and drags down everything around into the same degenerative process.

The crisply carved scenes of drama and struggle present vivid but crude pictures of victory and the destruction of the opposing forces of evil which constantly threaten the good. They are misleading, though, until they are balanced with other images of God at work and thus reinterpreted. Jesus' vision of the coming of the Father's kingdom when he saw 'Satan fall like lightning from heaven' (Luke 10:18) goes together with his vision of God's creative power working in secret, hidden places, like yeast in dough (Matt. 13:33). Divine power can be celebrated and trusted, yet it retains in this world the dimensions of vulnerability and precariousness, and includes the profound possibility that the cross may be not only the death of the Christ of God but also the final defeat of the divine creative energy and the collapse of meaning.

> Here indeed is the mystery which evokes our reverence, the mystery of the insinuation of timelessness into time, of immortality into the world of mortality. But that insinuation is not presented as achieving the defeat of the 'last enemy'. The enemy remains unconquered; that which we cannot visualise or imagine hangs over us all the time, death in which human existence runs into nothingness. If the poets enable us to lay hold on the uniqueness of words written and work wrought, their quality as intimations of mystery, they still leave unbridged the gulf between the relative and the absolute. No tapestry of metaphor, however marvellously woven, can render intelligible to us the end which awaits us all, or the manner of its overcoming, if, indeed, it is overcome.[48]

In the terrible pain and tragedy of our times, declaring and defining evil more vividly and searingly than any image can do, we are glimpsing the costliness of the process of creation both to God the Creator *and* to the human beings he is creating. Every parent remains to some extent 'in the dark' with his or her child both in youth and in age. In the language of a poster which appears in many car windows – 'parenthood is for life, not just for Christmas'. What we attempt to formulate in the words and images of poetry, in devotion and liturgy, and in doctrine is the ever-changing experience of trust between ourselves and God which cannot be boxed in and squared off, or ensured and guaranteed.

Trust within any partnership is the only bedrock on which to stand to find fulfilment, happiness and meaning, but it remains elusive, complex and perplexing. What can be said though, and what needs to be discovered is that the experience of trust at the heart of the relationship between ourselves and God affects *both partners* who *together* come to know the full range of the strength and the cost of the partnership. We have lost or not yet grown into an understanding of the relationship between God and humankind as equal partners in the process of being, with shared experience, comparable though different:

> … with every pilgrimage across strange and often savage landscapes, we also know that we are somehow coming closer to God's heart and purpose; with every step we are coming to a clearer understanding that his eyes are filled with tears just like ours.[49]

A human tendency is to separate and break things apart to gain understanding of them, while the divine purpose is to bring together and bind up. Breaking things apart as we do for analysis easily misleads, confuses and frustrates us, unless we go further and resynthesize them. Too often we leave separate what should be held in unity in spite of the struggle it is to do so. For instance, as we are considering now, no act of creation is possible without cost either to God or human beings. The meditations and prayers in the first section of this book (hopefully) provided a way of holding together both the achievement brought about by God in his creative work and what it costs him and us. God the Father carries the pain and agony of the world he has made in his heart as much as we carry it in ours.

> The cross in the heart of God from the beginning of time is a cross of creation as well as a cross of redemption. Or, rather, since the risk-laden process of loving into being is all of a piece, it is a cross of everlasting creative, redemptive and consummative self-giving.[50]

Maybe the cross is only 'a shaft of light' in the darkness, maybe there can be no floodlit truth. However, the unending invitation remains to be with God in the darkness and decide for ourselves whether his companionship provides light enough. Occasionally the light we need flashes suddenly and brilliantly, but more often meaning and knowledge are gathered slowly through much time and painful experience. Inevitably our relationship with God takes time to grow, strengthen and deepen.

There are signs to encourage us though, more readily available and closer than we realize, and from which those with little faith or a deepening faith can draw meaning. Thomas Traherne (1637–74) in his book *Centuries*, a remarkable collection of spiritual writings, pointed out that Christian faith is not far removed from our everyday life or so different from many experiences with which we are quite familiar.

I will open my mouth in parables: I will utter things that have been kept secret from the foundation of the world. Things strange – yet common. Incredible – yet known. Most high – yet plain. Infinitely profitable – yet not esteemed.[51]

We do 'die daily' and find sleep a health-giving process of renewal. We do go through periods of emptiness and withdrawal and discover that they are routes to fruitfulness and fulfilment. We do find in some cases that suffering leads to more than itself. There are examples of 'resurrection now' in people with whom we live and within ourselves. None of this *proves* the claim that life is stronger than death, but these experiences steadily reinforce the belief Christians hold, and they reveal that resurrection fits with what human beings already know, and is not a wild card or completely wide of the mark.

For example, George Herbert, another seventeenth-century priest and poet, went through times of collapse and renewal in his personal and private life. They are discussed in detail in an essay by L. C. Knights in which he describes Herbert's poem 'The Flower', which is almost certainly autobiographical and in which Knights finds 'that the sense of new life springing from the resolution of conflict is most beautifully expressed'.[52]

How fresh, O Lord, how sweet and clean
Are thy returns! ev'n as the flowers in spring;
To which, besides their own demean,
The late-past frosts tributes of pleasure bring.
Grief melts away
Like snow in May,
As if there were no such cold thing.

Who would have thought my shrivel'd heart
Could have recover'd greennesse? It was gone
Quite under ground; as flowers depart
To see their mother-root, when they have blown;
Where they together
All the hard weather,
Dead to the world, keep house unknown.

These are thy wonders, Lord of power,
Killing and quickning, bringing down to hell
And up to heaven in an houre;
Making a chiming of a passing-bell.
We say amisse,
This or that is:
Thy word is all, if we could spell....

And now in age I bud again,
After so many deaths I live and write;
I once more smell the dew and rain,
And relish versing: O my onely light,
It cannot be
That I am he
On whom thy tempests fell all night.

These are thy wonders, Lord of love,
To make us see we are but flowers that glide:
Which when we once can finde and prove,
Thou hast a garden for us, where to bide.
Who would be more,
Swelling through store,
Forfeit their Paradise by their pride.

George Herbert (1593–1633)

Considerable and worthwhile evidence is available, then,
that fruitfulness not sterility, abundance not paucity, life not

death, is God's desire and vision for his creation as much as it is our longing too; and one of the characteristics which makes God God is that what he desires he achieves.

> This word of the Lord came to me: 'O man, what is this proverb current in the land of Israel: "days pass and the visions perish"? Very well! Say to them: this is what the Lord God says: I have put an end to this proverb; it will never again be quoted in Israel. Rather say to them: The days are near when every vision will be fulfilled. There will be no more false visions, no misleading divination among the Israelites, for I, the Lord, shall say what I will, and it will be done. It will be put off no longer: you rebellious people. In your lifetime I shall do what I have said. This is the Word of the Lord God.'
>
> This word of the Lord came to me: 'O man, the Israelites say, "The visions which prophets now see are not to be fulfilled for many years: they are prophesying of a time far off.' Very well! Say to them: This is what the Lord God said: No word of mine will be delayed; whatever I say will be done. This is the word of the Lord God' (Ezek. 12:21–28).

No human being sees the action of Christ's rising; that remains God's secret. It had happened before the arrival of the first witnesses and, we may believe, while the soldiers were sleeping. But we know its results, and they are cause enough for Christian joy and our glad and willing disciple-ship as we discover them for ourselves. The fruits of the great action of divine love seen in the events of Jesus' resurrection and dying have still to be gathered. William Temple suggests that 'St John does not present them as a mighty act by which the hosts of evil are routed, but rather as a quiet rising of the sun which has already vanquished the night.' [53]

Death and Life have contended

At your resurrection that which is light and good rises up
     with you,
          and that which is heavy and evil is pushed downwards.
At your resurrection goodness breaks free from evil,
     life breaks free from death.

Adam of St Victor, Easter Sequence

The great fresco of the creation painted by Michelangelo on the ceiling of the Sistine Chapel in the Vatican has recently been restored. It shows God's energy and power bringing life to the world and to 'the first adam' – representing humanity. Most people who try to think of God as Creator usually begin with something like the same picture in their minds. For them Creation is divine *fiat*; 'God spake and it was done.' But because of the nature of the relationship between the Creator and his created beings and the kind of loving there is between them, in the last section we raised serious doubts about whether such a picture of God obscures more of the truth than it illuminates.

Jesus, when he thought of his Father's power as Creator, painted in a few words an equally vivid but utterly different picture. As he went towards his death, which for any Jew normally meant extinction or at the very best only rather a vague possibility of 'going on' afterwards (cf. Job 10:21–22),

Jesus said to Andrew and Philip: 'The hour has come for the Son of Man to be glorified. In truth, in very truth I tell you, a grain of wheat remains a solitary grain unless it falls into the ground and dies; but if it dies, it bears a rich harvest' (John 12:24).

Jesus appears to be suggesting that his death will become in God's hands not a disappearance into oblivion or a lifeless underworld but another way of coming to life. It will be a glorious event, a source of rejoicing rather like the annual harvest festival when 'all is safely gathered in'. Nevertheless, this process of coming to life will be very different from being born from the womb of his mother. Now Jesus must undergo at last a final act of creation at the hands of his Father, the faithful Creator, and he imagines the process in a simple yet profound way – like seed falling into the ground to receive from the darkness of God's good earth the gift of fruitfulness, fulfilment and completion.

After he had died Jesus went even further into the darkness. He went down into the depths of the earth. Like seed in soil, he endured a time of waiting which led to a process of renewal wrought by God which, with our almost totally inadequate language, we describe as 'resurrection' and the cluster of words around it which we struggle to use, like 'life renewed', 'new life', 'regeneration', 'life reborn'. Jesus reveals by his living and dying that the path to fullness of life must include times of seeding and growth, withdrawal and germination. Then with the boldest stroke of all, he asks us to think of death itself as part of God's overriding purpose of bringing his creation to birth.

Many poets, painters and preachers have shown Jesus' birth as a way of dying, or at least as belonging already to his approaching death. Plenty of Christmas carols picture the wood of the crib as the same wood as the cross. Now we are asked to look at it the other way round and consider another paradox. Jesus' death is a way of coming to life. He lies in the cradle already as it were looking far ahead:

Dreaming of Easter, gladsome morning,
Conquering death, its bondage breaking!

Here is the answer to Nicodemus' question, 'How is it possible for a man to be born when he is old? Can he enter his mother's womb a second time and be born?' Obviously not, but Jesus pointed Nicodemus to what can happen; and to what must happen. To reach the fullness of the Father's creation and to inherit its greatest gift, eternal life, all must be born 'of Spirit' as well as 'of flesh' (John 3:1–15). Jesus used the same image as his own inspiration as he approached his death. He went down into the waters of chaos to be born again, to receive his baptism by fire and the completion of his birth in the Spirit which began in the Jordan river.[54]

In the meditations we allowed our definitions of birth and death to explode and take on new shapes and dimensions. To identify ourselves with Jesus in his passion and dying, and experience how this kind of death brings resurrection, redefines what counts as beginnings and endings. What can look like a beginning, seen from certain view-points, is an end, and what looks like an end turns out to be another kind of beginning. To grasp this we need to understand Jesus' birth and death as a single action which cannot be separated and taken apart to find different meanings in each. Each aspect contains the same truth. Using technical, theological terminology, incarnation and redemption stand together as a single, united act of divine creativity, rather than apart, as two events in the divine programme of making and saving the world, separated by 'the Fall of Man'.

When Gerald Priestland went on his famous *Progress* for
the BBC a few years ago, one of the people he met was
Maurice Wiles, who was then Regius Professor of Divinity at
Oxford, who told him:

> I think the traditional accounts of Atonement and
> Redemption have tended to start with an assumption
> about Creation and Fall. They see Creation as something
> that was perfect in the beginning, which men then spoiled
> with their sins, and which at some point in history had to
> be restored to proper relationship by something dramatic.
> Now seeing the Creation and Fall as a story (I'll avoid
> using the word myth), I believe in Creation as something
> continuous that is going on all the time. So I see Redemp-
> tion as something that is going on all the time, as the
> fundamental character of God's creative activity. And I see
> the Cross as focussing this truth of God's reconciling love
> working for the harmony of his Creation.[55]

In other words, God's purpose is fulfilled in both his original will to create and his subsequent will to redeem, which
we should keep together as one unbroken act of creation. In
any case, if we can manage to think of God as eternal and
without time, then creation and redemption must be a single
movement of initiation and achievement through which God
reveals his love for all he makes and brings into being. It is
only the limitations of our methods of thinking which break
it up into moments of 'original' and 'subsequent' action.

There are, then, at least two contrasting concepts of the
Creator at work available to us. Whether we find meaning
and purpose in life, and whether we notice it or miss it,
depends very much on how in the first place we picture God
at work: spectacularly in divine *fiat* or more secretly and

hidden in mystery. The first picture of God is almost certainly less helpful than the second. Sudden, spectacular, almost dictatorial action in one who achieves his purposes easily and dramatically only conveys the beginnings of any knowledge of God. The other picture is much to be preferred. God's work within his creation is a quiet, mysterious process working itself out at incalculable cost and which lies for ever at the heart of all God ever makes and brings into being.

Humanity remains very close to the natural order and its processes because we are part of them. Natural growth with a process of birth, decline and renewal is provided by God to be the environment for human growth and development, both outwardly and inwardly, and it is a permanent and productive process in God's created order which can be trusted by all who share in it.

> While the earth lasts
> seedtime and harvest, cold and heat,
> summer and winter, day and night,
> shall never cease (Gen. 8:22).

In her notebooks the modern saint and mystic Simone Weil (1909–43) revealed that she was also reluctant to describe the power of divine creation as *fiat*. Instead she saw the seed of God's creative energy in what she called his 'loving self-renunciation', by which she meant his willing acceptance of suffering, a willingness revealed to its greatest extent in the death of Jesus. She wrote of God's self-emptying in taking the form of a slave in Christ; and for her, creation, the passion, and the Eucharist were all aspects of this movement of God's withdrawal and self-abandonment so that his creation can reach its full potential. Like a parent who stands back to enable the child to be, creativity for God is loving self-renunciation.[56] We can speculate to our heart's content about whether or not God has any other kind of power available to him, but we do know that lovingly he draws us towards fulfilment by his own self-giving, which turns out to be the actual power – the only power – which can properly be labelled 'almighty' because it is the energy which brings the divine Creation into being and to its full fruitfulness.

Simone Weil described the two ingredients in the mysterious process of our coming to God and our being open enough to receive all he gives in creating us as *l'attention* and *l'attente*, meaning 'concentration' and 'waiting'. She believed concentrated waiting on God is the basic action in prayer which opens up and establishes God's sovereignty over his creation. Praying in such a way reflects the divine method of sowing, reaping and harvest, and thus harmonizes and becomes at-one-with the creative Source bringing all life into being and completion.

> I warn all Inquirers into this hard point to *wait* – not only not to plunge forward before the Word is given them, but not even to paw the ground with impatience. For in a deep stillness only can this truth be apprehended.[57]

Simone Weil deliberately chose to live among the poor, while Thomas Merton (1915–68), another spiritual guide for us in the twentieth century, chose to live in solitude, but he also found the action of divine creativity in much the same place.[58] He called it *le point vierge* (literally, the virgin point), an image of the interior life we receive and enjoy in the Spirit through discipleship, through which both the presence and the activity of God are known and fulfilled.

The vision and purpose of all our efforts to be Christians and follow Jesus are to find and enjoy relationships which are fulfilling and spacious enough to have room for self and others, and for God. Human nature is designed for such large horizons and God in Christ is for ever creating these satisfying spaces within all who are growing in the Spirit. The divine method of bringing them into being is not domination but establishing ordered-being within chaotic-being, replacing sterility with fruitfulness, enabling the kingdom of love and forgiveness to defeat the terrible circles of power at work in the world and make them subject to God's 'just and gentle rule'; and the most useful image for us to picture God's providence at work and his sovereign rule being exercised over creation is the one used by Jesus, taken from the natural order of seedtime and harvest.

Thomas Merton believed that this God-centred work of creating is not only a past event but also a continuing action:

> Every moment and every event of our life on earth plants something in our soul … Every expression of the will of God is in some sense a 'word' of God and therefore a 'seed' of new life. If I were looking for God, every event and every moment would sow, in my will, grains of God's life that would spring up one day in a tremendous harvest.[59]

Those who allow themselves to be silent, to pray, and to be used and energized by God, and serve him constantly in the service of others, come to a new quality of life. Then they discover that the creative power bringing them to this kind of living is nothing less than the Father's resurrecting love known and declared in his Son, our risen Lord.

Within its own methods and definitions, which are very different from human concepts of power, the creative self-giving love of God remains for ever a powerful and irreversible source of energy within the world. Though all it brings into being must pass through a time of decay and death, nevertheless nothing it creates and redeems can be held by death in a destructive grasp. The resurrection of Jesus and the suffering and death which led up to it reveal and set in motion the costly completion of this process of creativity. Even though hampered and constrained, the power remains working and opens up and declares the true nature of reality whilst bringing it into being. To call such power 'almighty' is no longer to misuse a word but accurately to describe the resource and strength given to those who follow Jesus and live with a love like his, which is never self-demanding but endlessly self-giving. Through such discipleship God comes to us and we come to him. Then already, and within the darkness and sorrow of the world as it is, we awake with praise.

Notes

1. Paul Iles, *Touching the Far Corners* (Bible Society, 1996).
2. Michael Ramsey, *The Resurrection of Christ* (Geoffrey Bles, 1945), p. 7.
3. Quoted in John V. Taylor, *The Christlike God* (SCM Press, 1992), p. 47.
4. Frances Young, *Face to Face* (T & T Clark, 1990), p. 204.
5. John V. Taylor, 'The Future of Christianity' in *The Oxford Illustrated History of Christianity* (OUP, 1990), ed. John McManners, p. 641.
6. Probably Michael Ramsey knew this sentence in C. K. Barrett's *Commentary on St John's Gospel* (SPCK, 1958), p. 61: John understands [Jesus'] death to represent at once his plunge into the depths of humanity and his ascent to the glory of the Father.'
7. Alan Ecclestone's well-known book *Yes to God* (Darton, Longman & Todd, 1975) has not yet been surpassed.
8. M. R. D. Foot, *Six Faces of Courage* (Eyre Methuen, 1978), Ch. 7.
9. Donald MacKinnon, 'Reflections on Donald Baillie's treatment of the Atonement', from *Christ, Church and Society* (T & T Clark, 1993), ed. David Fergusson, p. 115.
10. E.g., read George Herbert's poem 'The Flower' on p. 153 below.
11. R. S. Thomas, 'Pilgrimages' in *Frequencies* (Macmillan, 1978).
12. Julian of Norwich, *Revelations of Divine Love*, translated by Clifton Wolters, (Penguin, 1966), p. 28.
13. Cf page 127 below.

14. A brilliant and moving scene in Susan Hill's *In the Springtime of the Year* echoes the situation: 'In that time between the fading of moonlight and the rising of dawn, everything about her [Ruth] seemed curiously insubstantial and she felt herself weightless, as though she were in a dream. But the long grass at the side of the path brushed against her legs like damp feathers. The world was real enough' (Penguin, 1977, p. 46).

15. 'The eucharist is not a re-enactment of the Last Supper; it is is a fellowship meal with the risen Christ in whom we are one with the Father and have God the Spirit indwelling in our hearts, at which we look back with gratitude to the sacrifice which made this blessedness possible, and which gives us assurance of the greater blessedness to come. Only because of the resurrection are we in this situation; and so a eucharist which does not have post-resurrection existence as its axis is not a proper eucharist at all' (J. A. T. Baker, *Thinking about the Eucharist*, SCM Press, 1972, p. 56).

16. Bishop Rowan Williams in his book *The Truce of God* (Fount, 1983) offers a thorough and cogent corrective to such misconceptions, especially in Ch. 4 'Not as the world gives'.

17. T. S. Eliot, *Murder in the Cathedral* in *Complete Poems and Plays* (Faber, 1969), Part 1.

18. Sydney Carter, *Dance in the Dark* (Collins, 1978), p. 45.

19. Kenneth Stevenson, *Jerusalem Revisited* (The Pastoral Press, Washington DC, 1988), pp. 4–5.

20. Good Friday was first celebrated as a public festival in the fourth century. 'It was the development of Holy Week at Jerusalem in the late fourth century which transformed the Friday of the Paschal fast into Good Friday as we understand it. The full growth of Good Friday meant that the commemoration of the passion was detached from the unitive *Pascha* which eventually came to be designated the resurrection alone' (*New Dictionary of Liturgy and Worship*, ed J. G. Davies, SCM Press, 1986, p. 190).

21. Quoted in Alan Paton, *Apartheid and the Archbishop* (Jonathan Cape, 1974), p. 12.

22. E. C. Hoskyns and Noel Davey, *Crucifixion-Resurrection, The pattern and theology and ethics of the New Testament*, ed. Gordon S. Wakefield, (SPCK, 1981). From our point of view, it might have been better if he had coined the word 'Resurrection-Crucifixion'.

23. If we accept the version of Mark's Gospel which ends with nothing except bleakness, which is highly dramatic and probably deliberate, it is worth asking if, even so, it is an invitation to those who are already celebrating the resurrection to make sure their joy rests on much firmer foundations than hitherto.

24. Jürgen Moltmann, *The Crucified God* (SCM Press, 1974). Ch. 2 describes many of the ways in which we 'accommodate' the cross to make it acceptable.

25. Blaise Pascal, 'Evil is easy, and has infinite forms', *Pensées*.

26. St Augustine, *Confessions*, ed. Henry Chadwick (OUP, 1991), p. 124–5.

27. C. Robert Mesle, *John Hick's Theodicy* (Macmillan, 1991), pp. 60–61.

28. St Augustine, *The City of God*, Book 22.

29. Ibid.

30. Terrence Tilley, *The Evils of Theodicy* (Georgetown University Press, 1991), pp. 89–112.

31. C. Robert Mesle, op. cit., p. 11.

32. Dylan Thomas, 'Do not go gentle into that good night' in *Collected Poems*, (J. M. Dent, 1971).

33. 'Thereafter followed a magisterial reading of the Book of Job, particularly the "Speech out of the Whirlwind" (chaps. 38–41), where finally the Lord answers Job's long, dense series of complaints with a set of powerful arguments focused on creation. The essence of the divine speech concerns the structures and techniques of the creation of the world – in relation to which Job's personal problems are put into perspective and thereby diminished, theodicy being an evasion of such issues rather than an answer to them' (*Reading George Steiner*, eds. Nathan A. Scott, Jr and Ronald A. Sharp, (The John Hopkins University Press, 1994), p. 263).

34. T. S. Eliot.

35. Cf. Sheila Cassidy, p. 22 above.

36. Dostoyevsky, *The Brothers Karamazov*, Bk 5, Ch. 4. Notice particularly that his penetrating discussion of the problem of suffering and the moral dilemma it poses for faith is followed immediately by the famous parable of the Grand Inquisitor in which Jesus is represented as suffering and yet retaining the power of silent, forgiving love.

37. W. H. Auden, 'Song for St Cecilia's Day'.

38. Moltmann, op. cit., p. 49.

39. 'Primary contact for Steiner is both more modest and more risk-laden. It requires from the reader less an intellectual than an aesthetic commitment, a willingness to 'tune oneself!' to the artwork and thus become part of the text's glorious problem rather than its solution. In short, we have come into primary contact when, one way or another, we fall in love with a piece of art and are moved to expand on its value in ways that expose our own vulnerabilities before it' (*Reading George Steiner*, op. cit., p. 75).

40. John V. Taylor, *Weep Not For Me* (World Council of Churches, 1986), pp. 11–12.

41. The point was made powerfully in a sermon preached on BBC Radio 4 in Lent 1995 by Frances Young and further explored in her meditation for Good Friday printed in *The Art of Performance* (Darton, Longman & Todd, 1990), p. 187.

42. George Steiner has urged passionately that we should return to the habit of reading primary sources rather than secondary sources about them. He wants us to read books, as he puts it, rather than books about books and, significantly, he goes on to underline that this is itself 'an act of commitment and risk' *Real Presences* (Faber, 1989), p. 8.

43. 'Page duBois' book *Torture and Truth* is one of a number of recent studies that perceive an affinity between truth-seeking discourse and the practice of extracting secrets under bodily duress or bringing about hidden knowledge to light through

techniques of physical coercion' (Christopher Norris, *The Truth about Post Modernism* (Blackwell, 1993), p. 257 and the notes attached to the text).

44. From Dennis Potter, 'Seeing the Blossom', a television play.

45. David Jenkins, 'God's Messages and God's Messengers' in *Bishops on the Bible* (SPCK, 1994), p. 56.

46. Gerald Priestland, *My Pilgrim Way* (Mowbray, 1993), pp. 118–119.

47. Among the many contemporary attempts to put this theme into narrative, perhaps the Narnia stories by C. S. Lewis are one of the most successful and attractive.

48. Donald MacKinnon, 'Reflections on Mortality', *Themes in Theology* (T & T Clark, 1987), pp. 83–4.

49. Tom Davies, *Landscapes of Glory* (SPCK, 1996), p. 107.

50. Peter Baelz, 'Why did God not make a better job out of it?', *Church Times*, 3 Dec. 1993.

51. Thomas Traherne, *Centuries*.

52. L. C. Knights, *Explorations* (Penguin, 1964), pp. 128–38, esp. p. 136.

53. William Temple, *Readings in St John's Gospel* (Macmillan, 1945), p. 375.

54. Cf. Psalm 69. Flesh and Spirit correspond to nature and the kingdom, two aspects of the divine creativity, and until both are brought to harvest, God's work of creation is in process rather than complete.

55. Maurice Wiles, in *Priestland's Progress* (BBC, 1981), p. 87.

56. Annice Callahan, *Spiritual Guides for Today* (Darton, Longman & Todd, 1992), p. 81.

57. Cf. St Augustine, quoted in George Steiner, *Real Presences*, p. 224.

58. 'My own peculiar task in my Church and in my world has been that of the solitary explorer who, instead of jumping on all the latest bandwagons at once, is bound to search the existential depths of faith in its silence, its ambiguities, and in those certainties which lie deeper than the bottom of anxiety. It is clear to me that solitude is my vocation, not as a flight from the

world – but as my place in the world' (Annice Callahan, *Spiritual Guides for Today*, p. 100).

59. Op. cit., p. 108.

List of Acknowledgements

'A brighter dawn is breaking' by Percy Dearmer from *The New English Hymnal* © The Canterbury Press Norwich.

'It has been a long journey' © the estate of Siegfried Sassoon.

'Travelling the Road to Freedom' from *Enemy of Apathy* © the Wild Goose Resource Group, 1988.

Quotations by Brother Roger are taken from the annual Taizé calendars.

'I believe ...' from *Livros de Cantos* © the Methodist Overseas Division. From *Bread of Tomorrow*, compiled by Janet Morley and published by Christian Aid, 1992.

'Interruption to a journey' from *Selected Poems*, published by the Hogarth Press, © Norman MacCaig, 1982.

Quotation from *In The Springtime of the Year*, published by Penguin Books, © Susan Hill, 1974 and 1989.

'The dark doubts of the winter months are past' by Katherine Middleton, from *Liturgy of Life*, ed. Donald Hilton, published by NCEC, 1991.

'When the hour comes' © Julia Esquival. From *Bread of Tomorrow*, idem.

'It's darker now, but there is light within us' by Lucy M Green, from *Liturgy of Life*, idem.

'Come on, Let us celebrate' © Elsa Tamez. From *Bread of Tomorrow*, idem.

'Risen Jesus, we thank you for your greeting' © John Johansen-Berg. From *Bread of Tomorrow*, idem.

'Let joy break out, eternal God!' by Donald Hilton, from *Liturgy of Life*, idem.

'God, you invite us to dance in delight' © Jan Berry. From *Bread of Tomorrow*, idem.

Extracts from *It was on a Friday morning* by Sydney Carter © Stainer & Bell Ltd, London, 1960.

'There was no cross cross enough' from *Assembled in Britain*, published by Marshall Pickering, © Stewart Henderson, 1987.

'Never shall I forget that smoke …' Extract from a BBC Radio 4 broadcast. Details not known.

Extract from 'God is love: let heaven adore him' by Timothy Rees © Mowbray & Co. Ltd.